ideals
COUNTRY

More Than 50 Years of Celebrating Life's Most Treasured Moments

Vol. 58, No. 3

How it comes back, that hour in June when just to exist was joy enough!
—Thomas Bailey Aldrich

Featured Photograph 6	Devotions from the Heart 33	Legendary Americans 54
Country Chronicle 10	A Slice of Life 36	Traveler's Diary 58
From My Garden Journal 16	For the Children 44	Handmade Heirloom 64
Remember When 20	Through My Window 48	Readers' Reflections 72
Collector's Corner 24		Bits and Pieces 82
Ideals' Family Recipes 26		Readers' Forum 86

IDEALS—Vol. 58, No. 3 May MMI IDEALS (ISSN 0019-137X, USPS 256-240) is published six times a year: January, March, May, July, September, and November by IDEALS PUBLICATIONS, a division of Guideposts. 39 Seminary Hill Road, Carmel, NY 10512. Copyright © MMI by IDEALS PUBLICATIONS, a division of Guideposts. All rights reserved. The cover and entire contents of IDEALS are fully protected by copyright and must not be reproduced in any manner whatsoever. Title IDEALS registered U.S. Patent Office. Printed and bound in USA by Quebecor Printing.

Printed on Weyerhaeuser Husky. The paper used in this publication meets the minimum requirements of American National Standard for Information Sciences—Permanence of Paper for Printed Library Materials, ANSI Z39.48-1984.

Periodicals postage paid at Carmel, New York, and additional mailing offices. POSTMASTER: Send address changes to Ideals, 39 Seminary Hill Road, Carmel, NY 10512. For subscription or customer service questions, contact Ideals Publications, a division of Guideposts, 39 Seminary Hill Road, Carmel, NY 10512. Fax 845-228-2115.

Reader Preference Service: We occasionally make our mailing lists available to other companies whose products or services might interest you. If you prefer not to be included, please write to Ideals Customer Service.

ISBN 0-8249-1167-9 GST 893989236

Visit *Ideals*'s website at www.idealspublications.com

Cover
Hollyhock display in Kewaunee County, Wisconsin
Darryl Beers, photographer

Inside Front Cover
A YOUNG GIRL IN A FIELD
Ludwig Knaus, artist
Hermitage Museum, St. Petersburg, Russia/Bridgeman Art Library, London/SuperStock

Inside Back Cover
SAY A NICE HOW DO YOU DO TO YOUR UNCLE
Carl Larsson, artist
Stapleton Collection/Bridgeman Art Library, London/SuperStock

NEW ENGLAND JUNE

Bliss Carman

These things I remember
Of New England June,
Like a vivid daydream
In the azure noon. . . .
Gardens full of roses
And peonies a-blow
In the dewy morning,
Row on stately row,
Spreading their gay patterns,
Crimson, pied, and cream,
Like some gorgeous fresco
Or an Eastern dream.

Nets of waving sunlight
Falling through the trees;
Fields of gold-white daisies
Rippling in the breeze;
Lazy lifting groundswells,
Breaking green as jade
On the lilac beaches
Where the shore-birds wade.
Orchards full of blossom
Where the bobwhite calls

And the honeysuckle
Climbs the old gray walls;
Groves of silver birches,
Beds of roadside fern
In the stone-fenced pasture
At the river's turn.
Thrushes in the deep woods,
With their golden themes,
Fluting like the choirs
At the birth of dreams.
Fireflies in the meadows
At the gate of night
With their fairy lanterns
Twinkling soft and bright.

Ah, not in the roses,
Nor the azure noon,
Nor the thrushes' music,
Lies the soul of June.
It is something finer,
More unfading far
Than the primrose evening
And the silver star.

A garden on Nantucket Island is a delight to the eyes.
Photo by William H. Johnson/Johnson's Photography.

Summer Comes

Stella Craft Tremble

From the hill comes radiant Summer,
Oleander in her hair,
Flinging sprays of jacaranda
As she mounts her golden stair.

On her cheeks the glow of primrose;
Lips are lush as purple grapes,
Weaving bands of pink mimosa
For the clouds she softly drapes.

Throwing moon-blanched sands behind her,
Sun-kissed honeysuckle sweet;
Now she rounds the full-fruit season
As she hastens to retreat!

Wrapped in hyacinthine twilight,
Holding soft winds in her hand,
Cloaked in rain and crowned with sunshine,
Summer leads her saraband!

Summer Is Here

Bess Harris

Here flares a flame of poppy red beside the pure white rose,
And fresh upon the tangled vine the honeysuckle blows.
The whippoorwill's far-sounding call falls from a wild plum tree
And mingles with the sweetest notes of little children's glee.
The sweet and tender clover blooms in fields of red and white
Where tiny dewdrops glisten in the early morning light.
The pirate bee is on the wing with pilfered honey-hoard;
The dance of moth and butterfly, the luna overlord.
The sun drops golden kisses upon the yellow rose;
The wind softly caresses where pinkish larkspur grows.
The rare and perfect days have come, gay season of the year.
Summer, gorgeous summer, once again is here.

RIGHT: *A simple trellis is enlivened by nasturtium blooms in this photo by Cliff Hollenbeck/International Stock.*
OVERLEAF: *Summer visits Pugh's Mill in North Little Rock, Arkansas. Photo by H. Abernathy/H. Armstrong Roberts.*

The Last Day of School

Eleanor B. Campbell

A hundred years,
Unending years
Of sweet anticipation.
The ocean sends
And shore extends
Enchanting invitations.

A thousand miles,
Unending miles
Of forest trails and sun;
A restless sea
And spirits free
To leap and skip and run.

Oh, gift sublime!
A summertime
Begins; and on this day,
This day of dreams,
September seems
A hundred years away.

School Vacation

Rudolph N. Hill

With last bells rung, all classwork done,
The long, long term of school is ended.
All minds turn toward vacation fun
With glorious thoughts of nature blended.

All out-of-doors speaks metaphors
Of life before a house was builded,
And arbor leaves of groves of trees
By light of dawn or sunset gilded.

The mountain's cool, the deep-woods pool
Re-echoes shouts and song and laughter
As when earth, young and beautiful,
Was not shut out by roof or rafter.

In silence dwell, O school and bell,
Through lovely, happy summer hours!
No words are adequate to tell
What one may learn from trees and flowers.

Two friends enjoy the barefoot days of childhood. Photo by Stephanie Rausser/FPG International.

Country CHRONICLE
Lansing Christman

SUNDAYS IN THE SUN

I have yet to find a summer long enough to give me all I want of those quiet Sundays in the sun. I am intimate with the acres around me, the meadows, the gardens and fields. I have worked in them, so I know them well. But on Sunday afternoons, I like to relax in the dooryard—to take in more of the summer sun, or to seek the cooling shade under the maples and the elms.

On such afternoons I take inventory of summer's ways, noting the progress of the season and the year. Birdsongs are fewer now than they were in spring, but the fields are maturing and the gardens are rich with color. The cows and ponies browse through the wild slopes of the pasture and along the lush marshes where the moisture holds. The kindness of the slopes imbues me with a contentment for life in the country.

My philosophy is nourished by these days of sun upon the fields, by the ripening hay and grain, by the slow step of livestock across the pasture, by the song of the field sparrow, the chirping of crickets, and the rasping notes of cicadas from the dooryard trees. Like the tendrils of the grape reaching for the haven of the trellis, I reach for every moment, holding on tightly to these Sundays in the sun.

The author of three books, Lansing Christman has contributed to Ideals *for almost thirty years. Mr. Christman has also been published in several American, foreign, and braille anthologies. He lives in rural South Carolina.*

Miniature ponies spend their Sunday afternoon on a hillside pasture in southeastern Pennsylvania. Photo by Londie G. Padelsky.

An Old Rail Fence

Agnes Davenport Bond

Winding about on the side of a hill,
An old rail fence is standing there still.
The cross-barred rails, now darkened with age,
Appear like a scene on an old tattered page.
The days of one's childhood are brought back to mind,
When fences like this were all one would find.
Picturesque yet, on the side of the hill,
A memory picture is standing there still.
But time makes its changes as years pass away;
And what we are seeing before us today
Perhaps may seem old in the years that are hence,
As old and untimely as this weathered fence.

To a Rail Fence

George McDonald

Companioned by the chipmunk and the wren,
The woodchuck and the pheasant mother-hen;
Arms interlocked against the common foe,
By country roads, zigzagging down they go.
Between the rails wild roses intertwine,
Sweetbrier roses and trailing berry vine.
And from the top rail bobwhite sends his call
Across the silent meadow where the tall
Green grasses, fanned by summer breezes, sway.
Though vanquished by the enemy, decay,
In memory they are not far away.

A rail fence frames the scenery from Buckhorn Viewpoint in Wallowa County, Oregon. Photo by Steve Terrill.

Journey Into Joy
Grace V. Watkins

For unadulterated joy,
Go find a sunlight-seasoned boy
Companioned by a line and hook,
A rustling willow, and a brook.
Notice the basket wide and high
With mounds of sandwiches and pie.
Linger a while and you will feel
A half-forgotten wonder steal
Into your grown-up heart and glow
With deep content from long ago.

Along the Pasture Stream
Gail Brook Burket

The future and the past have wandered here
And paused to skip smooth stones with dextrous care
Or watch a dragonfly's blue crinoline
Cut crisply through the static summer air.
How do we know the future and the past
Were mirrored in this pool where sun nets gleam?
Recorded in warm sand are ageless prints
Of barefoot boys along the pasture stream.

Two young brothers head for a day at the fishing hole in Mom Won't Mind *by artist Kathryn Andrews Fincher. Image copyright © Arts Uniq, Inc., Cookeville, Tennessee.*

From My Garden Journal

Lisa Ragan

SNAPDRAGON

Snapdragons earn a place of distinction on my list of all-time garden favorites as easy-to-grow plants with a long season of colorful blooms. But snapdragons not only charm the hearts of flower gardeners; they also capture the fancy of little children, vegetable gardeners, and bumblebees.

During the carefree summer days of my childhood, I could most often be found barefoot in my sandbox. I was fond of creating sand castles and inventing elaborate tales of the princes and princesses who lived within their walls. When our next-door neighbor Jackie came out to do her gardening, I often ran over to greet her and follow her around for a while. Every summer she grew a magical little plant called a snapdragon. The first time she showed me how to pinch the snapdragon's "cheeks" to make it open its "mouth," I was captivated. Back at my sandbox, I was soon saving the villagers from the ferocious snapdragon in my sand castle legends.

While this hardy, flowering beauty is busy kindling the imagination of a four-year-old, the snapdragon also helps to ensure a successfully pollinated vegetable garden with a resulting bounty of crops. The secret? Bumblebees! Bumblebees have the brute force necessary to push themselves into the classic snapdragon blossom and drink the hidden nectar, whereas honeybees don't have the strength even to enter the blooms. Some modern varieties of the snapdragon have more open blossoms that can be entered by honeybees or bumblebees. But since bumblebees lack the capacity to store a substantial amount of the precious nectar and need a readily available supply for their survival, they cannot handle much competition. Vegetable gardeners plant traditional varieties of snapdragons, such as the Rocket variety, to encourage bumblebees to visit their garden. The bumblebees in turn help to pollinate crops such as tomatoes, squash, peppers, and melons, which may mean bigger and more plentiful vegetables to harvest.

Native to the Mediterranean, the snapdragon was also popular with ancient Russians for the oil that could be cultivated from its seeds. This oil was prized by the Russians and compared in value to olive oil. The snapdragon became a favorite throughout England in the sixteenth century, but was sometimes referred to by the names Lion's Mouth or Calf's Snout, the latter because of the seedpod's resemblance to a calf's snout.

SNAPDRAGON

Traditional snapdragon plants produce spires up to four feet tall with tubular blossoms in a variety of colors encasing the top third of each spire. Solid color options include purple, red, orange, pink, salmon, yellow, and white—almost any color but blue. Bicolored snapdragons are also available in a whole range of colors.

The modern snapdragon can be found in tall, medium, and dwarf varieties, with tall plants reaching to the four-foot range and dwarf varieties stretching to only eight inches. The taller varieties may require staking with dried bamboo or small branches when the plants reach their full height. Rocket hybrids produce classic snapdragon blooms with the lipped tubular form while the butterfly hybrids (also called azalea-type hybrids), such as Madame Butterfly, produce a more open blossom. The velvety blossoms can be found in double and single forms and can be smooth or ruffled. Snapdragon scents range from a sweet, candy-like fragrance to a more spicy, almost cinnamon-like aroma.

The snapdragon is often mistakenly considered an annual, but in truth it is a tender perennial that will survive the winter in any region where the temperature does not dip below 10° F. In these moderate regions, snapdragon seeds can be planted in autumn and the young plants will survive the winter months. For colder climates, seeds can be germinated indoors in mid-February. The tiny seeds of the snapdragon need several months of growth to produce plants hardy enough to withstand a final frost or two. Sprinkle the seeds over a growing medium and simply press down with the bottom of a juice glass. It is not necessary to cover the seeds. Another option is to purchase tender, young snapdragons from a local nursery and plant them in well-drained soil a few weeks before the last frost of the year. Choose a sunny spot and water the plants when the soil feels dry. Other planting locations to consider include the crevices of rock walls or in between paving stones, since snapdragons can tolerate somewhat dry, rocky soil. Gardeners often find that their snapdragons will self-pollinate and naturalize in the garden.

Profuse blooms of vivid color thrive during the spring and early summer months but will wither as the weather turns warmer. Depending on the heat and level of humidity of the summer climate, snapdragons may stop blooming altogether. Gardeners can, however, snip the plants down to the soil level in the heat of summer and then enjoy another round of spectacular blossoms come autumn.

Snapdragons make an excellent addition to a cutting garden since the more blooms you cut for your indoor enjoyment, the more blooms they will produce. Be sure to snip any dead blossoms regularly to encourage additional blooms. These hardy little bloomers have few problems; but tender, new shoots can prove irresistible to hungry aphids. Spraying soapy water on the shoots periodically should control any aphid infestations. Snapdragons can also succumb to rust disease, but check a local nursery for varieties that have been bred to resist rust.

Even though I've long since outgrown my sandbox, I haven't outgrown the joy of watching children discover the magic of snapdragons. As I pinch the snapdragon's cheeks for my little neighbor Joseph, I thrill to see his eyes widen in surprise when the snapdragon "bites" his finger. Perhaps he'll treasure this memory too and one day grow up to sow snapdragons in a garden of his own.

Lisa Ragan tends her small but mighty city garden in Nashville, Tennessee, with the help of her two shih-tzu puppies, Clover and Curry.

Hill Farm Reclaimed

May Smith White

I must reclaim this land that others knew,
For here bright hopes were kept alive for years.
I also feel some would expect me to,
Knowing this soil has always conquered fears.
In hurried manner once this place was sold
Because the yield was small at harvest time;
And too, the graying house was getting old,
For through the years each thing had lost its prime.
But strangers cannot know how this farm grieved
As when they walked along each wooded trail.
And neither can they know the pattern weaved
By those who love these hills fenced in by rail.
I must redeem, from strangers now, this land,
Or I will feel a silent reprimand.

THE HERITAGE

Marvin Davis Winsett

These rock-strewn hills that I once knew as home
Are cherished ground. The heritage of birth,
Where long ago my plowshare sliced the loam,
Is mine by right of kinship with this earth.
I took my bread from this unwilling sod;
With my bare hands I labored here to yield
A meager gain and fought the weed and clod
From row to row across the stubborn field.

The creaking trace-chain on the singletree
Was pleasant to my ear. The scent of clay,
Freshly upturned, comes back again to me.
These things the years can never take away.
While age has dimmed the memory of toil,
My hands still long to feel remembered soil.

A hill farm in Block Island, Rhode Island, is crowned by a sky full of clouds. Photo by William H. Johnson/Johnson's Photography.

THRESHING DAY

Marjorie Holmes

For children raised in city or suburbs, there is nothing more fascinating than a farm. Practically all our relatives lived on farms, and both my parents had been born in the country. Our favorite cousins to visit were the Pattens, distant relatives on Mother's side.

Even if we had already spent our allotted time on Patten's Farm, we were always invited back for threshing. Partly to share in the heady drama of this major event of the summer, but also to help. Cooking for threshers must be experienced to be believed. The very term has come to signify something Paul Bunyanesque, gargantuan. A thresher doesn't eat a mere serving of potatoes, he downs the whole bowl; nor a piece of pie or cake—at least half of it, sometimes all, plus maybe an entire jar of pears or peaches. For a full week before the onslaught of threshers, every available hand was welcomed for the preparing of fruits and vegetables, the cooking and baking.

My sister and I pitched in, along with an assortment of married daughters who came home with fat babies to be nursed and diapered and added to the general atmosphere of urgency, confusion, and celebration. For this was the first step of the harvest season. The corn, "knee-high by the Fourth of July," now stood a tall, green, rustling forest higher than a man's head. ("Don't go out in it, kids, you could get lost.") It must await its hour of picking and husking in the fall. But already there had been two cuttings of alfalfa, and now the oats were ready. Ripe in mid-July, they had been cut, the bundles dotting the landscape like a candlewick spread. Then, as if Indians had come in the night, the bundles had been piled into tepee-shaped shocks. Now all these little wigwams were to be gathered and delivered of their precious grain.

The man who owned the threshing machine usually came the night before. Excitedly we awaited the arrival of that mighty dragon in the dusk. At last there came a puffing and clanking down the road, a smell of smoke, a glitter of sparks as the steam engine that hauled it turned into the lane. Like a great leashed beast it followed, bigger than a fire engine and more imposing, with its belts and wheels and gears and platforms and mighty stacks. . . .

The teams and wagons and hayracks began arriving shortly after sunrise, driven by the men from five or six neighbor families who belonged to the threshing ring. The whole barnyard became a hubbub of activity that rivaled the circus in its lively, lusty noise. Harnesses jangled, wheels creaked, horses whinnied and sometimes reared, men's voices called and kidded. Empty hayracks rattled off to the fields and came back slowly, fat and groaning with their whiskery load. The machine, now primed and roaring for its task, was fed and began to spew out its separate products: straw in golden blasts, a sandy pile of chaff, while into the wagons flowed a steady silken river of the grain.

The wagons then were pulled into the open-ended granary; and there, under its pitched roof, the teams were maneuvered over the complex machinery of an elevator, which would carry their slippery cargo in buckets to be tipped into the bins. Outside, another team of horses plodded in patient circles merely to keep the shafts and gears and belts and chains in motion. . . .

Everything had to be cooked and ready and on the enormous table with its checkered cloth by noon. Home-canned pork and beef swimming in gravy; fried chicken; four or five kinds of vegetables; mountains of potatoes; pickles, relishes, jelly; staggering bowls of coleslaw; hot biscuits and cornbread and thick slabs of white bread (some men made sandwiches of everything within reach); pie and cake and rice pudding,

Farmers break from their labors to enjoy a bountiful country table in this photo by Grant Heilman.

plus applesauce and peaches and berries and cherries. Everything crammed bowl by jar by jowl to save both time and room. (Nobody waited for courses or for each other.)

Outside, the ravenous men would have consulted the thick nickel watches in their overall bibs and begun watering their horses before the first shift headed toward the wash-house. There, itching with straw and grain, they stood around awaiting their turn to wash from the chipped white basin set on a wooden bench. . . . Then, like great ruddy beasts to be fed, the first shift came clumping into the kitchen. The food disappeared with incredible speed into their seemingly bottomless pits and was replaced again and again. Full at last, they sauntered into the yard to josh while the second batch took its turn.

On threshing day women got dinner all morning and washed dishes and got supper all afternoon. But it was all lively and rich with talk and purpose, and somehow festive—the click and clatter of bone-handled knives and forks, and the heavy ironstone plates, brown-bordered with a fleur-de-lis in the center, most of them as checked and lined as the faces of the women who handled them.

Supper was more fun, like a party. Though some of the men had gone home to do their chores, others worked until dark. And when at last they trooped wearily into the lamplit kitchen, they often found their wives, who'd come bearing further food. More plates were squeezed onto the already crowded table. Bone-tired as everybody was, a sense of rejoicing and celebration prevailed. More coffee was poured; more pies were cut.

All that food! All that plenty! A sense of the overflowing bins and barns was in the air. A sense of reaping some vital harvest, not only of the crops but of human effort. Friends and neighbors linked together in a common triumph. The success of this day was the success of them all; and tomorrow it would be repeated down the road, and next week somewhere else. So the harvest didn't stop here; the harvest moved in a perpetual ring of helping and sharing.

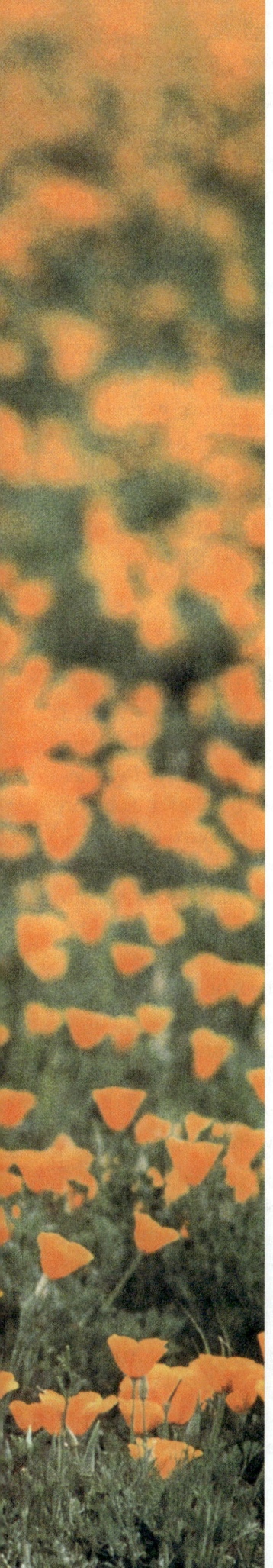

Misplaced Country Girl
Lois Fears

The city's no place for a country girl.
She doesn't enjoy the rushing whirl,
Nor the noise in the street all night,
And neighbors so close, both left and right.
Oh, what she'd give for a chance to look
Over a meadow and wade in a brook;
Pick dogwood blossoms in the spring,
And see the wild birds on the wing;
Hear a whippoorwill's call on the evening breeze
As it whispers softly through the trees;
And walk through woods when leaves are turning.
These are the things for which she's yearning.

Come Summertime
Sandra Lytle

My country friend, I'm thinking of you now
As spring is brightly bursting on the bough
And wishing I could be with you somehow
To stroll down lilac lanes that we once knew.

Here in the city, we have daffodils,
But ah, I miss the lush green, rolling hills;
And ivy twining to the windowsills
That brought such pleasure when I was a child.

I long for country roads that slowly wend
To lilting streams that lie around the bend.
And peaceful places where a heart can mend
Like meadows all aglow with buttercups.

Oh, yes, my friend, I'm thinking now of you,
With envy, as some city girls will do.
So plant an extra sunflower or two,
'Cause I'll be country bound come summertime.

A country girl strolls among the poppies. Photo by SuperStock.

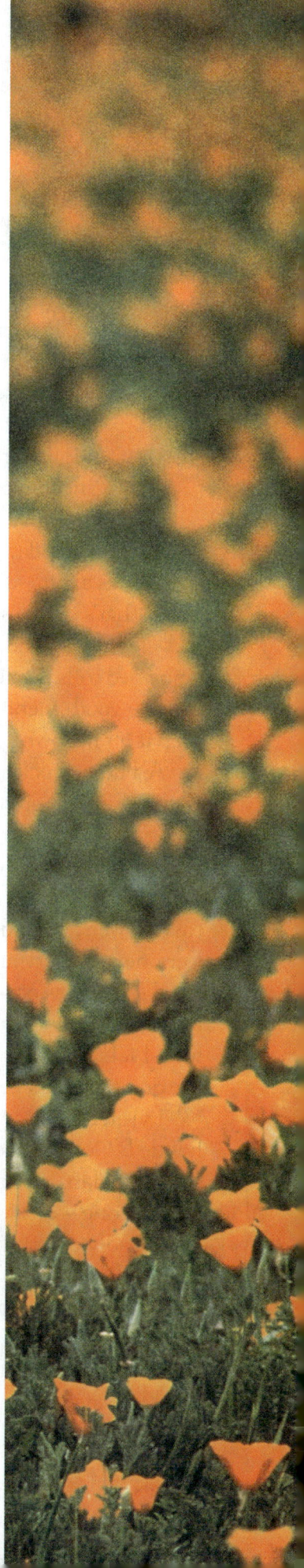

Collector's Corner

Butter Crocks

Laurie Hunter

A friend of mine makes excellent homemade yeast rolls—the soft, comforting kind that make you feel as if all's right with the world. So naturally, a hard brick of butter to accompany them just won't do. Instead she keeps a tub of butter on the table for smooth spreading. But the commercially packaged tub, which is not much for looks, never seems to do the rolls justice.

For her birthday, I found the perfect solution to give her as a gift—a wonderful, cobalt blue pottery piece that's just as carefully and lovingly made as her renowned rolls. If she were not such a good friend, I might keep it for my own collection!

A butter crock was always present on my grandmother's lazy Susan that sat center stage on her breakfast table. Whether serving bowls heaped high with steaming oatmeal or platters of silver-dollar pancake towers, Grandmother made sure the plates were never empty and the butter crock was always full. I grew up associating a butter crock with a plentiful spread. So of course when I became a newlywed, I felt our table must have one to complement the domestic bliss I envisioned cooking up.

I visited a few antique malls but came up empty handed. Out of sheer stubbornness, I stuck to my original plan of finding a butter crock until I located one—or a second-rate excuse for one. It was a badly chipped, blue spongeware butter crock that had faded to a dismal gray. My husband took one look at it on our table and declared it absolutely unappetizing. If my goal was to represent comfort and hospitality, I knew I had not yet achieved success.

This kick-off to my collection was functional but hardly aesthetically pleasing. As any collector knows, the best pieces combine function with beauty. So my search for a fitting butter crock became a quest.

Ironically, although butter crocks were created to keep butter cool and fresh before refrigeration was invented, I discovered that they're sought after as hot collectibles even though refrigerators are now as commonplace as butter crocks once were. Over the course of many years of visiting local antique shops on Saturday mornings, I found several butter crocks that now congregate in an interesting cluster on a shelf in my hutch. My collection today includes butter crocks that both grace the sideboard and earn their keep.

One avocado-green ceramic pot is encircled with, fittingly, a butterfly motif. Another crock is made from red enamelware speckled with white. My yellowware butter crock is nearly twice as big as the others and bears no decorative patterns or glazes, but it makes up for any plainness with its rich, buttery golden hue. My favorite, a prized Rockingham crock, sports a unique brown, drizzled glaze; its lid is missing, but it still retains a place of honor on the shelf with the others as a handy storage bin for mismatched, antique butter knives.

For everyday use, I store butter in a much newer, seemingly simple white butter crock in the refrigerator, placing it on the table an hour or two before the meal. My china is white as well, so, to the indiscriminate eye, the butter pot joins the place settings as if it came with the service.

I view the butter crock as an unassuming American icon that can turn a modern meal into a comforting family ritual. Perhaps my friend will agree. Like the rolls she insists on painstakingly making herself rather than buying at a supermarket, the butter crock I'll give her for her birthday is proof that living in a modern world doesn't have to mean surrendering all the comforts of a simpler time.

> *I view the butter crock as an unassuming American icon that can turn a modern meal into a comforting family ritual.*

Butter Up

If you would like to collect butter crocks, the following information may be helpful.

History

- Before the refrigeration of food, perishables such as butter easily spoiled. To prolong its shelf life, butter was stored in crocks and kept in the cellar, springhouse, or well box.
- Early butter crocks were made of wood and covered with cloth. These wooden bins were difficult to clean and prone to breed bacteria.
- By the end of the eighteenth century, redware crocks with tight-fitting lids became available from potters in one- and two-gallon sizes.
- Stoneware crocks became the butter storage pots of choice by the mid 1800s, when many sizes, styles, and designs were manufactured.
- By the late nineteenth century, butter crocks were turned out using decorative molds or adorned with sponged patterns, freehand designs, or special glazing techniques.
- Commercial dairies stocked grocery stores with butter by the twentieth century, decreasing the need for butter crocks. But many people continued to make and store butter in crocks at home.

Hints for Beginners

- Crocks are typically made from ceramic materials, including pottery and stoneware with or without glaze.
- You may want to select one type of butter crock to collect, such as pots made by a particular potter, crocks bearing advertising messages, or highly decorated crocks.
- Butter crocks without their lids aren't as prized as more intact versions.
- When searching for crocks, consider the weight of the pottery and thickness of its walls. Both help to keep the butter cool.
- Though not as valuable as a pot in mint condition, a crock with imperfections, chips, or dents can have character, especially if you know the piece's history.

A collection of simple butter crocks awaits its newly churned treasure. Photo by Jerry Koser.

Usage and Care

- Today butter crocks should not be used as a replacement for refrigeration. Use the crocks to store butter inside the refrigerator, relying on them to keep your butter fresh on the table only for a few hours.
- Be sure to check for lead or other toxic chemicals (with a do-it-yourself test kit) that may have been used in the pot's glazing process. If anything hazardous is discovered, use the butter crock for decorative purposes only, or place a plastic or glass dish inside it to serve as a liner.
- Don't rinse unglazed crocks, since immersing them in water may cause swelling or cracking. Wash glazed crocks by hand with a mild soap.
- Over time, glazes on ceramic pieces tend to develop a crackled pattern due to excessive or prolonged moisture. These cracks, known as crazing, do diminish the piece's value, so use favorite collectibles for display purposes only and store in dry areas.
- As with any ceramics, sudden temperature changes may cause pieces to break.

Ideals' Family Recipes

Try packing your next picnic basket with something a bit more clever than your everyday fried chicken and potato salad. Each of these recipes is quick to prepare and requires few ingredients—perfect for a spontaneous trip to the park. We would love to try your favorite recipe too. Send a typed copy to Ideals Publications, 535 Metroplex Drive, Suite 250, Nashville, TN 37211. We pay $10 for each recipe published.

Stromboli Salad
Mrs. Marlene Puler of Alexandria, Virginia

1 1-pound box small seashell pasta
¾ cup cubed provolone cheese
¾ cup thinly sliced pepperoni
¾ cup cubed ham
1 cup chopped tomatoes
¾ cup chopped green pepper
½ cup chopped onion
½ cup finely chopped black olives
1 8-ounce bottle Italian salad dressing

Cook pasta according to package directions. In a large bowl, combine pasta with remaining ingredients. Chill. Makes 12 to 16 servings.

Black-Eyed Pea Salad
Wilma Hudson of McDonough, Georgia

2 16-ounce cans black-eyed peas, drained and rinsed
½ cup chopped onion
2 tablespoons Dijon mustard
¼ cup lemon juice
3 tablespoons olive oil
½ teaspoon dried oregano or thyme
Black pepper to taste

In a large bowl, combine peas and onion; set aside. In a small bowl, combine remaining ingredients. Pour over pea mixture and mix well. Chill. Makes 8 servings.

Confetti Sandwiches
Dorothy Rieke of Julian, Nebraska

1 6-ounce package grated Swiss cheese
¼ cup finely diced green pepper
⅔ cup salad dressing
12 slices dark rye bread

In a small bowl, mix first 3 ingredients. Spread bread slices thickly with tablespoons of cheese mixture. Makes 6 large sandwiches.

Poppy Seed Chicken Salad
Michelle Lasley of Brentwood, Tennessee

4 tablespoons granulated sugar
1 teaspoon salt
4 tablespoons vinegar
½ cup vegetable oil
½ teaspoon pepper
4 chicken breasts
3 green onions, chopped
⅛ cup poppy seeds
½ cup sliced almonds
½ cup rice noodles

In a small bowl, combine first 5 ingredients and chill overnight if possible. In a large saucepan, boil chicken breasts 20 minutes or until cooked. Rinse in cold water, then chop. In a large bowl, combine chicken, green onions, and poppy seeds. Add dressing. Chill 4 hours. Before serving, add almonds and rice noodles. Makes 4 servings.

Sour Cream Rhubarb Pie
Darlene J. Michalski of Marshfield, Wisconsin

3 cups chopped rhubarb
1 9-inch pie shell
1 egg
1 cup sour cream
3 tablespoons cornstarch
½ teaspoon cinnamon
1¼ cups granulated sugar
Non-dairy whipped topping

Preheat oven to 425° F. Place rhubarb in the bottom of the pie shell; set aside. In a medium bowl, beat egg. Add remaining ingredients and mix well. Pour over rhubarb. Bake 15 minutes. Lower the oven temperature to 375° and bake an additional 40 to 45 minutes or until golden. Serve with whipped topping. Makes 6 to 8 servings.

Down-to-Earth Things

Edna Jaques

The strong, clean smell of yellow soap,
A farmer plowing with a team,
The taste of huckleberry pie,
A pan of milk with wrinkled cream.

An orchard where sweet apples grow,
Their rosy cheeks turned to the sun,
A meadow sloping to the creek
Where long sun-dappled shadows run.

And all about the farm there lies
A peace that townfolk never know,
A woman happy and content,
A quiet field where old trees grow.

A little boy plays in the yard
Under the shade of an old tree
His granddad planted long ago
For little boys that were to be.

A graveyard up the road a bit,
Where their forefathers gently sleep,
While these—the living—go their way
The blessed things of earth to keep.

A day full of down-to-earth things is pictured in Sweet Meadowland *by artist Linda Nelson Stocks.*

Idiosyncrasy
Sheila Stinson

His methods are unusual,
Although in shining rows
Are cabbages and beets and peas,
The things a gardener grows.

But tucked between each homely thing
You'll find a marigold,
A zinnia or coralbell
Wherever space will hold.

This gardener's heart lifts with delight
As tiresome hoeing looms
When interspersed along the rows
Are pink petunia blooms.

Petunias
Georgia B. Adams

Spilling over the windowbox,
Petunias gay!
With every straying playful breeze
They nod and sway.

All summer long they laugh and lift
Each fragile cup,
Greeting the golden sun above
And looking up.

Cool white and pink, they bend to greet
The passerby.
Somehow it seems I almost hear
Their tender sigh.

Lovely they are! What heart does not
Enjoy their stay?
Spilling over the windowbox,
Petunias gay!

Petunias overflow a barn-side garden plot in this photo by H. Abernathy/H. Armstrong Roberts.

Devotions from the Heart

Pamela Kennedy

But the Lord is my defense; and my God is the rock of my refuge. Psalm 94:22

ROCK SOLID

The summer I was fifteen, my mother decided she and I should take a three-week road trip from Seattle to a small town in Missouri to visit my mother's youngest sister. My father had to stay home to tend his business. He assured us he would have plenty to keep himself busy in our absence since he was planning to put a patio in our small backyard. The day we piled into our 1956 Dodge to begin the trip, I remember my mother kissing my dad good-bye and saying, "Now, don't overdo. Keep it simple, honey. We just need a place for the picnic table." He assured her he would take care of everything, and we drove off filled with expectation.

After an exciting three-week journey, we arrived home late one night, unloaded the car, and fell into bed exhausted. By the time I woke up, the sun was streaming into my room. I hopped out of bed and, still in my pajamas, went out to the kitchen. The back door was open, and I could hear my parents' voices drifting through the screen. As I rounded the corner into the backyard, I stopped and stared. The yard was transformed!

Extending from the back of the house was a gently curved slab of concrete edged with rows of marigolds and purple petunias. A short pathway of bark chips led from the patio to a circular area cut out of the lawn and filled with smooth, round river rocks. And in the middle of this rocky island stood a large boulder. It was about three feet high and roughly two feet by two feet at its flat top. Perched upon this rock in her bathrobe, my mother sat sipping a cup of coffee and looking adoringly at my father.

"What in the world is that?" I asked, pointing at the boulder.

Mother chuckled and took Daddy's hand. "It's my rock. My refuge."

At fifteen, I had no idea what she was talking about, but in the ensuing years I learned. My mother was a quiet woman who enjoyed solitude. My father and I were noisy extroverts who viewed silence as a vacuum needing to be filled with noise. In his loving understanding, my father had recognized the need of his wife to have a place of her own to be alone, even if it were only within the confines of our small backyard. As the years passed, I often saw my mother retreat to her rock, sometimes sitting in the sunlight, absorbing the warmth from the granite beneath her. At other times, she stole out at night and contemplated the sky from her stony perch. That rock became a metaphor for home when I moved away—the solid, unmovable place where things could be still and secure.

When David wrote of God as his rock and refuge, I believe he was thinking of a similar image. Life is uncertain. Things and people change. Relationships and loyalties realign. We need a place where we can know stability and security. God, in love and grace, provides that place in Himself. He remains the same regardless of our circumstances. In Him we can take refuge from the noise and confusion of life. Where do you go when you need to find peace? Scripture reminds us that the security and serenity we seek is only a prayer away.

> *Dear Lord, thank You for being my rock and my refuge. Help me to always find my way to You when I'm feeling lost or confused.*

Large boulders add a focal point to the landscape in this summer garden.
Photo by Jessie Walker.

A Father Is a Strange Thing

Robert P. Tristram Coffin

A father is a strange thing—he will leap
Across a generation and will peep
Out of a grandson's eyes when unexpected,
With all the secrets of him resurrected.

A man is taken by complete surprise
To see his father looking from the eyes
Of a little boy he calls his own,
And thought he had the breeding of alone.

His father looks direct through eyes new blue,
His father moves on stout thighs quick and new,
He takes hold of things as once he did,
And none of his old handsomeness is hid.

The grace the father thought well hid away
Shines like the sun upon a boy at play;
The love he kept so close for none to see
Looks up naked at the father's knee.

All the proud, high ways his father had
Are lowered to his knee. A man is sad
To see them so, but then he catches breath
To see how one so loved has cheated death.

*T*HERE IS NEVER MUCH TROUBLE IN ANY
FAMILY WHERE THE CHILDREN HOPE
SOMEDAY TO RESEMBLE THEIR PARENTS.
—WILLIAM LYON PHELPS

Favorites of Father are gathered in this vignette by photographer Nancy Matthews.

A SLICE OF LIFE

Edgar A. Guest

Art by Eve DeGrie

BEST TRIBUTE

He opened the door, and he shouted, "Hello!"
And a foot race to greet him began
With the happiest welcome that any can know
To gladden the heart of a man.

He lifted the winner high into the air,
And his hat was swept off to the floor.
As reward for the burdens a man has to bear,
No king could have anything more.

Three children to run to the door with delight,
Their love for their daddy to show.
So eager to see him—homecoming at night
Is the finest of tributes I know.

Edgar A. Guest began his illustrious career in 1895 at the age of fourteen, when his work first appeared in the Detroit Free Press. His column was syndicated in more than three hundred newspapers, and he became known as "The Poet of the People."

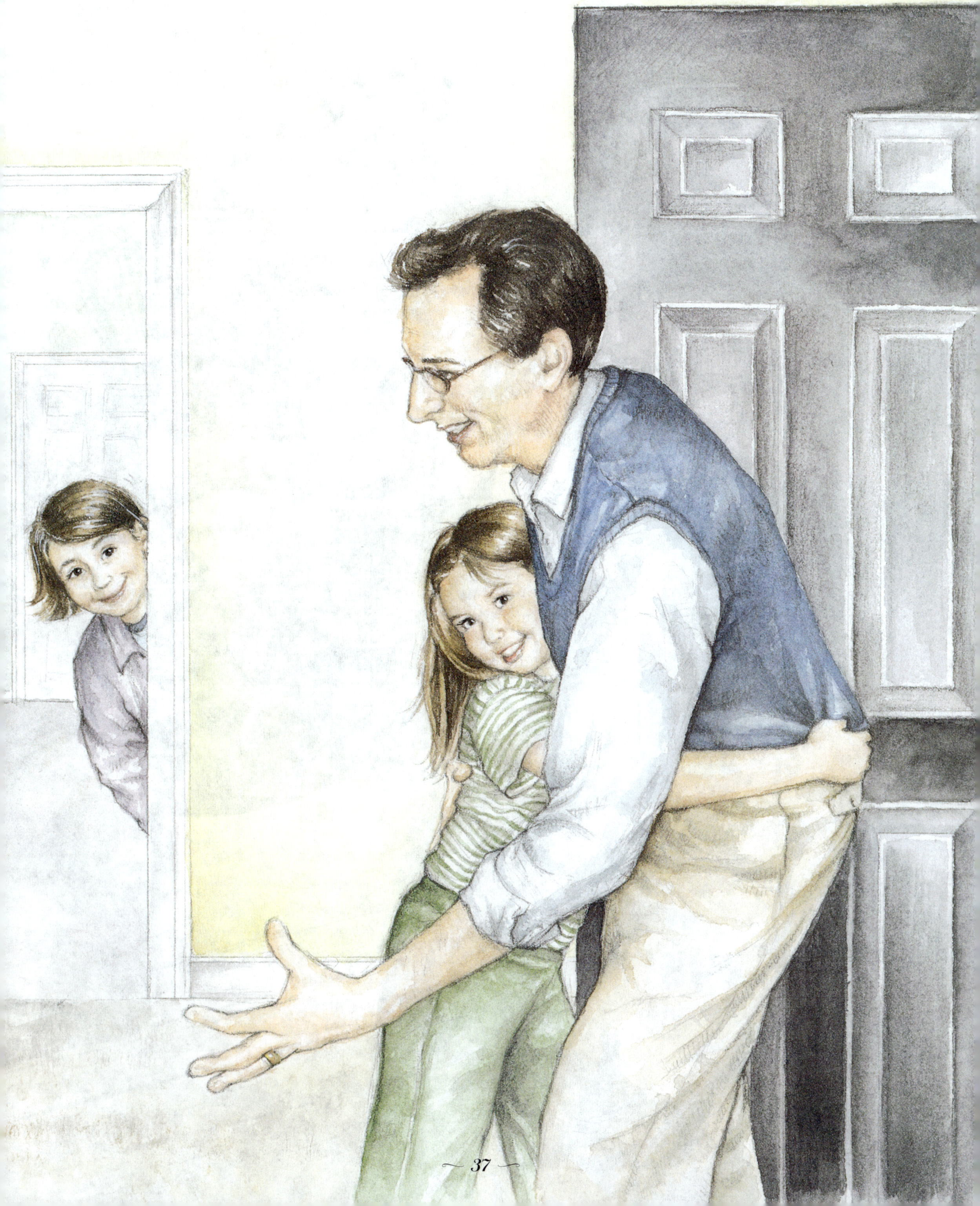

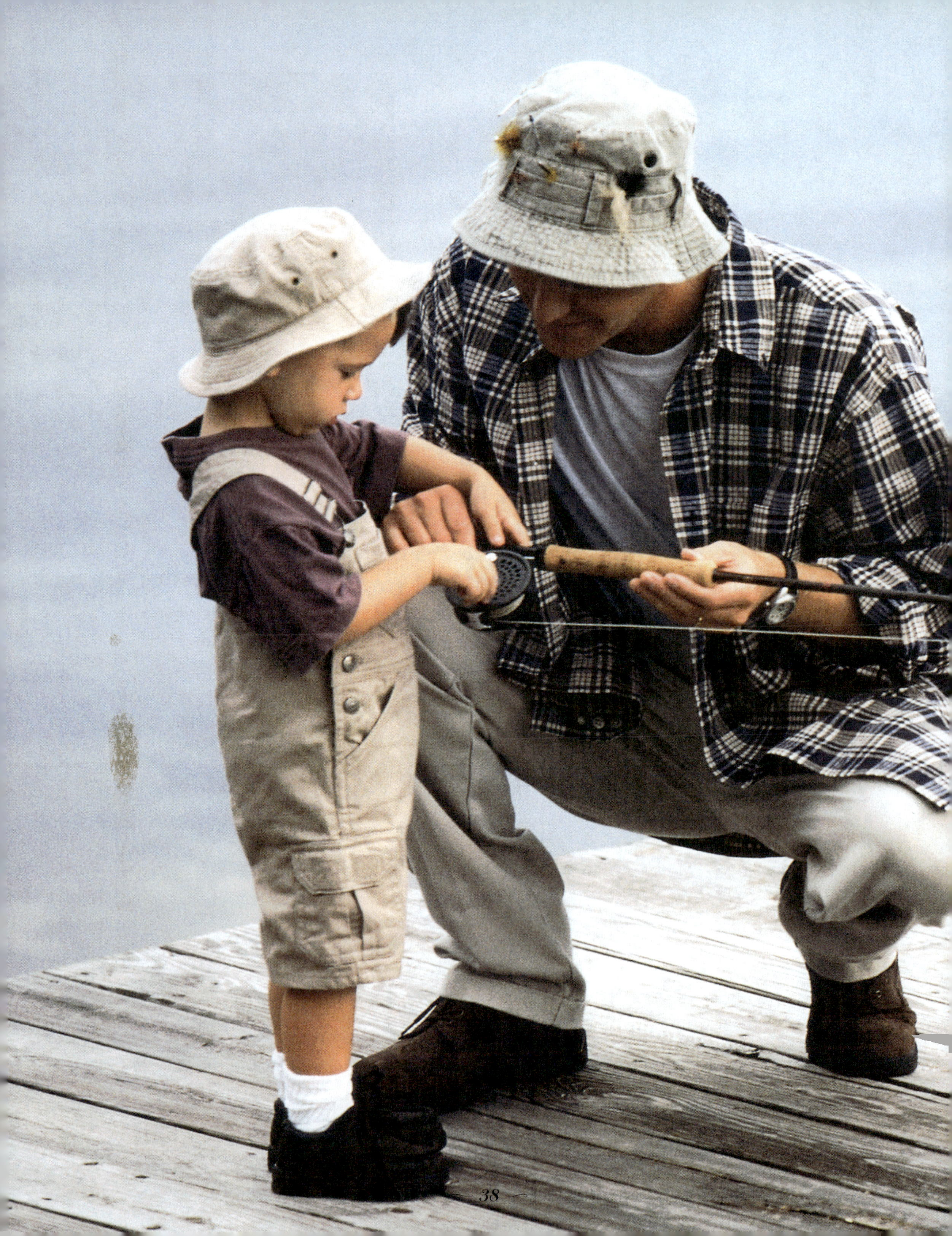

A Father's Prayer

Mauzon W. Brabham

Father, today I bring to Thee
This boy of mine whom Thou hast made.
In everything he looks to me;
In turn I look to Thee for aid.

He knows not all that is before;
He little dreams of hidden snares.
He holds my hand, and o'er and o'er
I find myself beset with fears.

Father, as this boy looks to me
For guidance and my help implores,
I bring him now in prayer to Thee;
He trusts my strength, and I trust Yours.

Hold Thou my hand as I hold his,
And so guide me that I may guide.
Teach me, Lord, that I may teach,
And keep me free from foolish pride.

Help me to help this boy of mine,
To be to him a father true;
Hold me, Lord, for everything,
As fast I hold my boy for You.

A father shares his know-how, and his love, with his son. Photo by SuperStock.

These tempting blackberries in Bristol, New Hampshire, would most likely never make it to the berry pail. Photo by William H. Johnson/Johnson's Photography.

SUMMER'S FOREST

Marilou Trask-Curtin

It seems now, upon reflection, that the summer of my ninth year was the very best of all. Trees then whispered more secrets, birds sang more gaily, skies were bluer, and the sun shone down in honeyed gold.

It was July when summer came alive for me that year—late July when the days gear down to a lazy, drowsy harmony and heat waves shimmer on the meadows. Even the breezes were hot. That year my Grandpa and I played many games of catch in the field behind the chicken coops. I ran and struggled to catch the ball that my still small but growing tomboy hands couldn't quite grip. When I did catch the ball, Grandpa would laugh, he would sparkle, it seemed; and the sunshine on his snow-white hair seemed to reflect halos around his gray-green eyes.

It was that summer that Grandpa burst into my still-darkened bedroom banging two cooking pots together. "Rise and shine, Johnny" (his tomboy nickname for me). "The blackberries are ripe, and your grandma wants to make some preserves. Let's get going before the sun gets too hot."

I rolled quickly out of bed, wiping sleepiness from my eyes, and got dressed. After a breakfast of warm oatmeal, I presented myself to Grandpa. Since this was the first time I was allowed to go berrying for preserves, Grandpa explained the process to me in detail while he got out the "berrying pails." These were two small tin pails with handles. Our belts were put through the handles and the pails were pulled around so Grandpa's was at his back and mine was on my side. Soon we were ready, and off we started.

The dew marked our path through morning's meadow. Birds chirped wake-up hellos, and the low-lying morning mist cooled, eddied, and flowed around us as we made a tunnel through it. When I looked back over my shoulder, the mist had closed like a gate behind us. I could see no signs of houses or shapes at all. We were wrapped in solitude. There was no talking. I remember feeling a oneness with Grandpa, with the forest, and with myself. Peaceful. The security of being in the fog, but of not being there alone.

Finally, it seemed like hours later, we came upon a bank of blackberries stretching on forever; a solid wall of briars hung heavy with juicy blackness, and we began picking. By noontime our buckets were full, and so were we. Berries tasted best right from the briar. I was sure it was time to head home and to the lunch Grandma would surely have ready, but Grandpa had other ideas.

"Let's hike around for a while, Johnny," he said.

Gripping my pail securely in my now purple-stained fingers, off we hiked. My stomach was suddenly very hungry and complaining at every step.

Deep, deep into the forest darkness we went, following the deer trails. The sun was directly overhead now, and despite the shadows of the cloistered pines, I was hot and sweating. My clothes clung to me in steamy moistness. As we trudged onward, the smells of the forest engulfed us in scents of decaying leaves and heavy pine. We often caught our pants on briars and limbs, and twice I almost fell face-forward on the trail.

Suddenly, without warning, Grandpa dropped out of sight!

"Grandpa!" I screamed. "Where are you?"

Then I heard the chuckling. Looking down a few feet away from where I stood, I could see just the top of Grandpa's snow-white head. He was sitting in a small pit and surrounded by thousands, it seemed, of his morning-picked blackberries. I crept closer to the edge of the pit and set my pail down on the rim. Grandpa reached up and lifted me down with him. We both reckoned that a deer hunter had dug out the pit as a deer trap years ago—and what a trap it had turned out to be!

We sat for a while in that quiet coolness, talking about this and that and listening to the lazy sounds of the forest around us. As we sat, hunger naturally got the better of us, so we ate the rest of the blackberries from my pail. As we ate, we gathered together our excuses to tell Grandma and then decided that nothing would work like the truth.

We climbed up and out of the pit and set our sights homeward. Once Grandpa stopped for a rest by an old oak tree, and as he sat down on the mossy ground, he spied a small pine seedling about eight inches high. I could tell by his grin that he had something in mind; and, sure enough, I didn't have to wait for long.

"Johnny," he said, "wouldn't that little tree make a nice gift for your grandma? Let's pull it out of there," he said as he rubbed his hands together.

So Grandpa got a grip on the little tree, and I got a grip on Grandpa's belt, and we tugged and tugged and tugged. Nothing. Once more we tried, and THUNK! We both fell backward and Grandpa victoriously held aloft the little pine seedling, roots and all. Carefully he wrapped it with some of its soil in his white handkerchief, and off we went for home.

We came upon a bank of blackberries stretching on forever; a solid wall of briars hung heavy with juicy blackness, and we began picking. By noontime our buckets were full, and so were we.

I can tell you now that Grandma was only mildly upset about her berries not being delivered. And late that afternoon Grandpa and I planted the little pine seedling. Oh yes, Grandma did get more berries the very next day.

It's been almost thirty years since that marvelous summer, and Grandpa's smile and Grandma's preserves are only memories now. But every day I have a living reminder right outside my kitchen window. The once-little pine seedling is now a tall and stately pine tree. And you know, over the years a most amazing thing has happened. From the one seedling, two trees grew together—one trunk is slightly larger, stronger, and tougher, and the other is smaller, dainty but strong. The small one has a slight lean in the direction of the other.

They both stand now as if my Grandpa and I were watching the pathway to the meadow, waiting to be together once again in a summer long ago, when trees whispered leaf-laden secrets, birds sang more gaily, and a little nine-year-old girl nicknamed Johnny ran off through summer's forest to go blackberrying with her grandpa.

THE HIGHEST REWARD FOR A MAN'S TOIL IS NOT

BUT WHAT HE BECOMES BY IT.

WHAT HE GETS FOR IT

A FATHER'S WISDOM

Emma S. McLaughlin

Remember how, when I was very young,
I stood beside you, Father, in the shop,
While busily you pursued a work you loved,
And I plied you with words I couldn't stop?
My questions often trivial to you,
When I asked them in the small alcove,
Were always answered gravely, thoughtfully,
Tempered with wisdom and a father's love.
I gained a wealth of knowledge at your side,
For as you carefully helped me with the wood,
You also offered me a set of rules
And guideposts for the road to adulthood.

"You always make a plan," I heard you say,
"Know what you are going to do before you start,
Then try to do the very best you can,
Give to it all your mind, your strength, your heart.
Finish it carefully, make rough spots smooth,
Strike each nail squarely, drive them straight and true,
So you can always know you've done your best
And sense the pride of full achievement too."

I don't think you only spoke of wood,
Spoke only of the job at hand to do;
I was so very young—you could not see
You pointed out a way of life for me.

*A woodcarver demonstrates the work he loves.
Photo by Unicorn Stock Photos.*

—JOHN RUSKIN

For the Children

Sprinkling
Dorothy Mason Pierce

Sometimes in the summer

When the day is hot,

Daddy takes the garden hose

And finds a shady spot;

Then he calls me over,

Looks at my bare toes,

And says, "Why, you need sprinkling,

You thirsty little rose!"

A "little rose" takes a delightful drink in the original oil painting SUMMER COOLER *by artist Donald Zolan. Copyright © Zolan Fine Arts, LLC. Ridgefield, Connecticut. All rights reserved. www.zolan.com.*

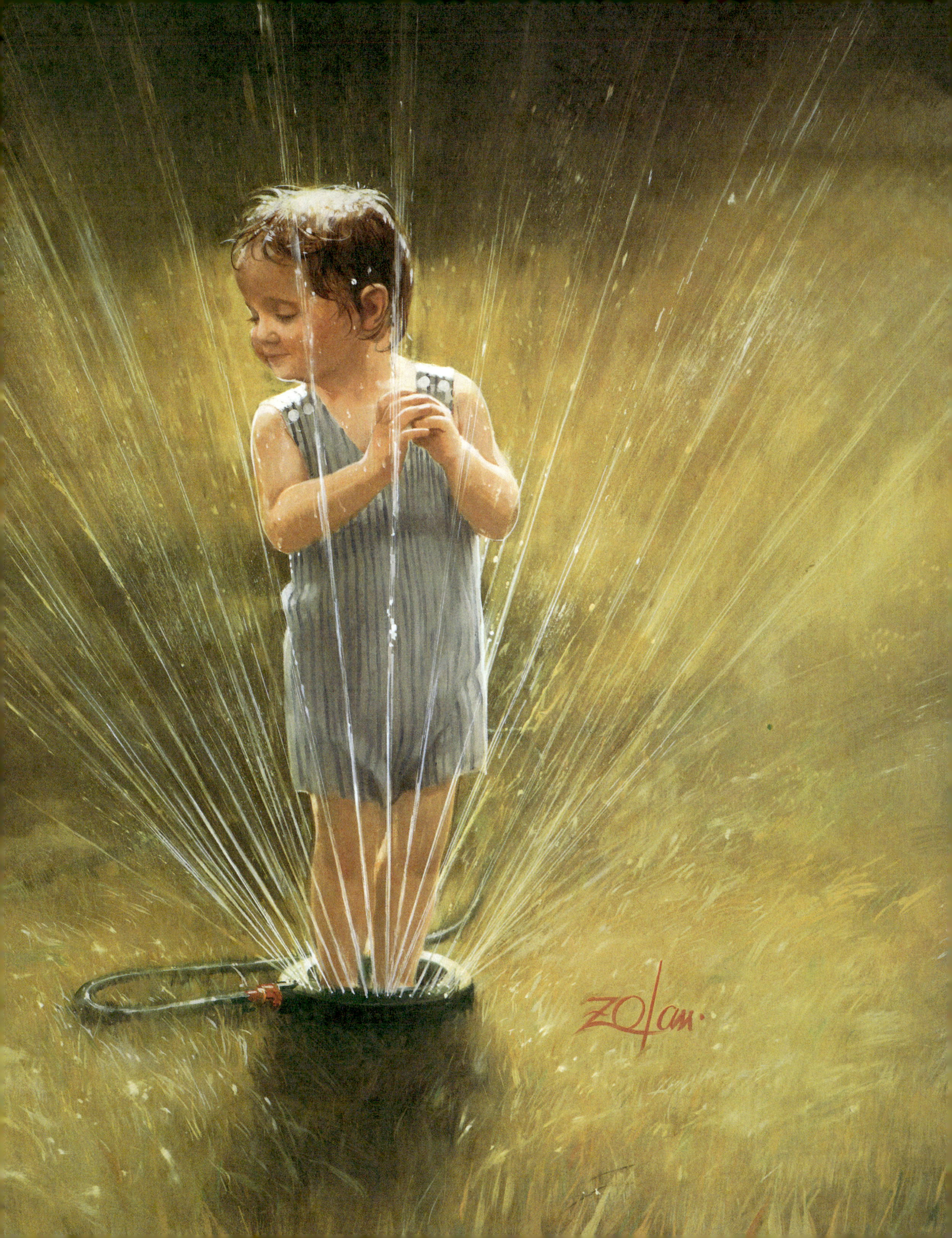
Zolan

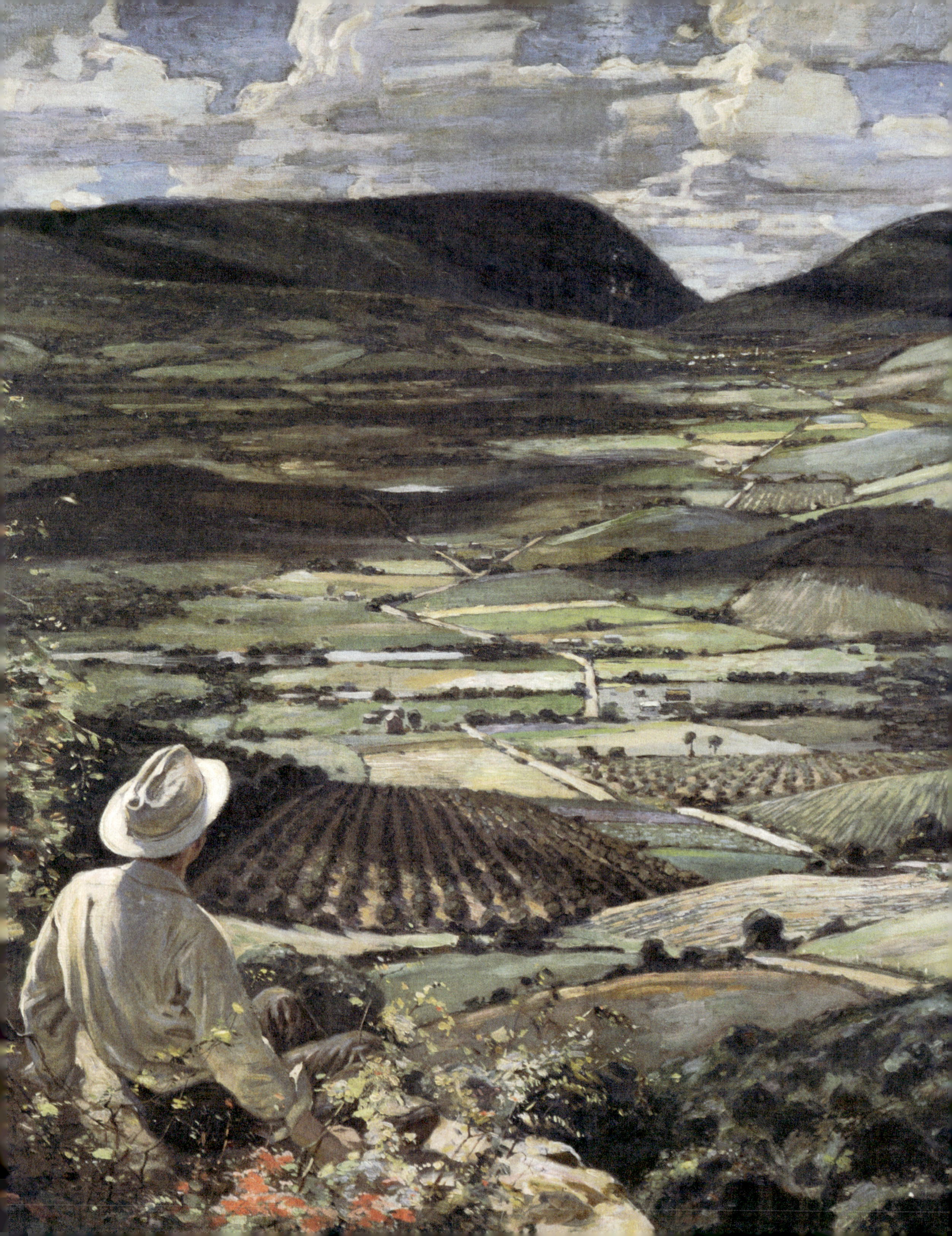

Portrait

Dorothy Miller Birdwell

He comes slowly from the field
At dusk on a summer evening,
Tired and weary from the day's work;
And over his shoulder he carries a hoe.
A man of the soil all his life,
He's known long hours, hard work,
Worn-out shoes, patched overalls, faded blue shirts,
And sometimes penniless pockets—yet he is rich.
Weather beaten and sun-burned face, calloused hands,
Skinned knuckles, sweat-stained brow:
He wears a countenance of strength and deep contentment.
He's battled the elements—sometimes won, sometimes lost—
But always he did the best he could,
Managed to survive and plan the next year's crop.
A quiet, gentle man with a deep love of the soil,
Plants that bloom, sunshine and rain, fragrant hay,
Fat cattle, sleek horses, and white-faced calves—
All their needs before he thinks of his own.
Always ready with a smile, to lend an ear or helping hand,
Solve a problem, fix a toy, to guide and teach, to show the way.
A big dog walks by his side.
A boy and girl run to meet him,
While under the big pine tree, waiting,
Stands a lovely woman.
Finished at last with the day's work
And coming home to supper,
This man with the hoe—
My father.

A farmer surveys his life's work in Valley View *by artist Martin Lewis. Image from Christie's Images.*

THROUGH MY WINDOW
Pamela Kennedy

Art by Meredith Johnson

MANGO MAMAS

When we relocated back to Honolulu after my husband's retirement from the Navy, we joined a large church. It was always hopping with some kind of project, program, or special event. When you are new, however, it is sometimes challenging to know where you fit in and difficult to feel connected by only attending services on Sundays. That's why when Alice, one of the ladies in our adult Sunday School class, announced that she needed mango choppers to show up on Wednesday to help make chutney for the women's bazaar, I decided to go.

Wednesday morning I grabbed an old butcher apron and a sharp paring knife and headed for the church kitchen. When I arrived, Alice was already there, directing action in the kitchen like a general overseeing the strategic planning of a critical battle. She had two stoves going full bore. On one, clouds of steam rose from roasting pans filled with boiling water and clattering mason jars. The other held a pair of eighteen-quart kettles filled with a bubbling fruit mixture. Spotting me as I peeked apprehensively around the corner of the doorway, she raised her wooden spoon like a saber and gestured for me to enter the "war room."

"Thank goodness, you brought your own apron and knife! This is Patty and Bambi and Mary and Lucille." She paused, pointing at me with her spoon. "Have you ever made mango chutney before?" I shook my head. Alice sighed. "OK, we'll start with something simple. We're making double batches, so we need lots of mangoes chopped. Go out there, and Auntie Ellen will show you what to do." She waved in the direction of a gray-haired woman who was wielding a serious-looking butcher knife. "Ellen, here comes your helper!"

Auntie Ellen, the obvious matriarch of mango chutney, looked me up and down like a drill sergeant ruefully examining a new recruit. "Well, come over here," she said, patting the empty chair next to her. Quickly, she set me up with a wooden cutting board and a box filled with green mangoes. "Here's what you do," she instructed. "Whack off the ends, then peel it like an apple, around and around. Then you slice the fruit off the seed, then you slice those slices into thin strips." To demonstrate, she deftly reduced a mango into uniform, matchstick strips. "Now you try."

I plucked a firm mango from the box. Carefully slipping my blade under the leathery peel, I began turning the fragrant fruit. Orange juice dripped down my fingers. When the peel was off, I proceeded to slice and then cut the fruit. Finished, I looked at Auntie Ellen for approval. From her expression, I assumed my mango peeling left something to be desired.

She lifted another mango out of the box. "We're going to try this again," she said patiently. "See that green stuff on your slices? That's bitter. See how you got too close to the seed? Makes stringy chutney. See how you got some fat strips and some skinny ones? Let's see if we can get 'em all the same size. Here." She plunked the mango into my left hand. Under Auntie Ellen's tutelage, I carefully corrected my mistakes until I was producing uniform slices without a trace of green. "Now you got it," she smiled.

After a while, we had pots of chutney bubbling on the stove. Scents of ginger, raisins, mango, onion, peppers, vinegar, and spices blended into an aromatic steam. And as the tangy fragrance drifted over us, the women began to "talk story." One octogenarian recalled how her mother used to pick mangoes, avocados, and papayas from the trees in their backyard and haul them to the public market on summer mornings, and how she used to go along to buy rice candy and pickled plums from Mr. Tomishiro at his corner shop. Another told about her uncle who came from China to work in the sugar cane fields in the early 1900s. Each month he sent his meager pay back to Canton, until he eventually managed to bring his brothers, sisters, and parents to Hawaii, where they all found work, raised their families, and established one of the most respected businesses in Honolulu. A younger woman mentioned a concern about her husband's health, and two others offered suggestions of a doctor specializing in such cases. Someone requested prayer for a son seeking a new job, and another had us giggling over an episode with a client at work. And all the while we peeled mangoes, chopped ginger root, stirred chutney, and filled jars.

I suspect that church kitchens all across the country have been witness to the same kinds of things. Women gather to make chutney, jam, pies, quilts, baby layettes, or crafts to sell at church bazaars. They raise money for missions and the homeless and other worthy causes, but in the process they create something else of great value. They build friendships. They reach out to one another with hope and encouragement, laughter and tears, breaking barriers of age and ethnic background.

In the sticky task of cutting up mangoes on a Wednesday morning, I discovered something that had eluded me during the majestic organ music and prayers of Sunday worship services. I discovered fellowship. In the middle of doing, I found devotion. And I am convinced that it is in this blending of heart and hand that our faith becomes real. Even in our churches it is easy to remain isolated, thinking we have little in common, feeling alone or even unloved. But when we work together for a common goal—even one as simple as making chutney—we connect with one another.

As I washed my cutting board, Alice gave me a pat on the back and thanked me for helping.

"Oh, it was really fun," I replied, picking a bit of fruit off the front of my apron.

"Yeah," piped up Auntie Ellen, as she wiped down a sticky counter, "and she did pretty well for a beginner. Of course I had to help her out some." She raised her shiny butcher knife in a jaunty salute and then laughed. "I think maybe she can be the newest Mango Mama!"

Pamela Kennedy is a freelance writer of short stories, articles, essays, and children's books. Wife of a retired naval officer and mother of three children, she has made her home on both U.S. coasts and currently resides in Honolulu, Hawaii.

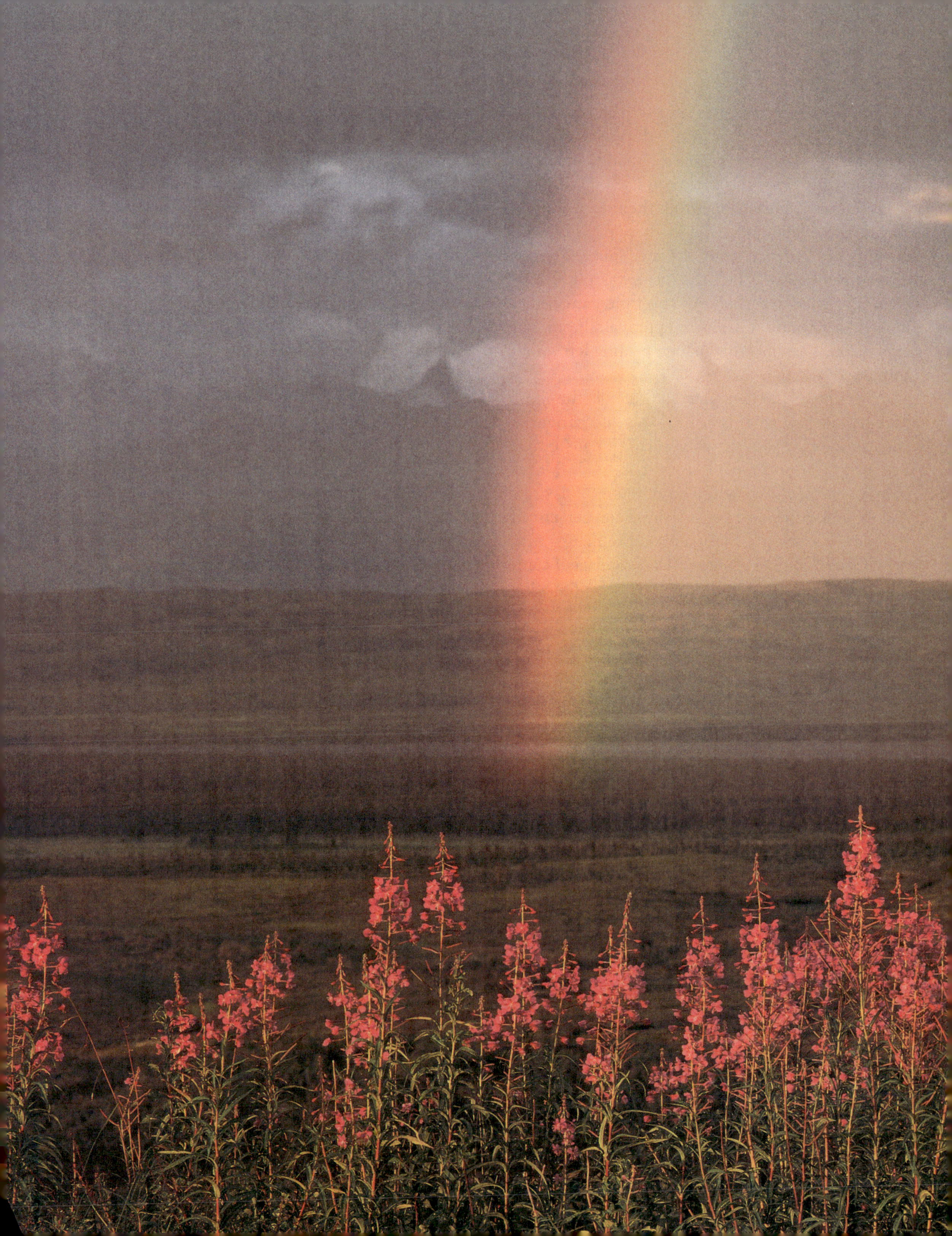

No Blue Can Match the Sky

Florence Pedigo Jansson

No blue can match the sky, no green the grass;
For petal tones of flowers, no copyright
Can be obtained; their depth and glow surpass
All human skill in molding grace and light.
Synthetic fragrance, mocking substitute
For souls of flowers, for sweetness gladly spent,
Can claim no depth of firmly anchored root
From which the rose derives its matchless scent.

No pulsing symphony that stirs the air
Can match the robin's song in simple grace;
No instrument, however famed and rare,
Can shame the meadowlark or take its place.
The splendid things, the things of truest worth
Are nature-formed, inherent in the earth.

Only Omnipotence

Jessie Wilmore Murton

Only omnipotence could think of these:
The stateliness of shimmering poplar trees,
Translucencies of blue and silver skies!
Only the Infinite could attune the cries
Of wild geese winging northward through the night!
Where is the skeptic's answer to the might
That with the glacier and the desert's brand
Scars earth's face, yet with the selfsame hand
Tints violets and pale anemones,
While night by night star-patterned mysteries,
By ages left unraveled, still declare
His glory who creates and holds them there;
And day by day the cryptic changing sod
Shows forth the delicate handiwork of God!

A rainbow arches over Denali National Park and Preserve in Alaska. Photo by Carr Clifton.

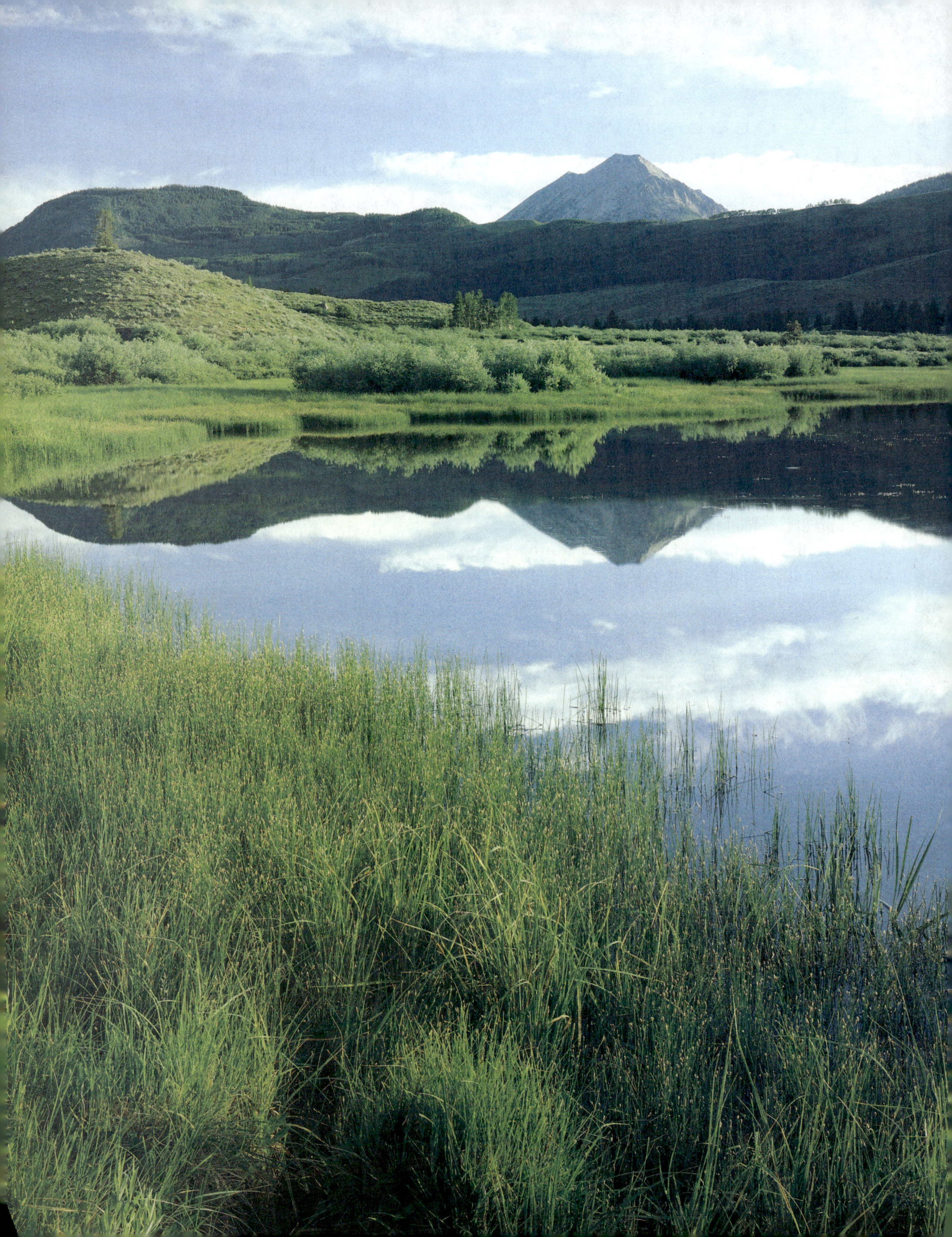

NATURE'S MIRROR
Gladys Harp

Nature has a magic mirror
That minimizes ours.
It duplicates the sun and moon
And multiplies the stars.

It frames a borderline of trees
And snowy mountain crest,
And windblown clouds are pictured
Where waterlilies rest.

There is no landscape painting
More pleasing to the eye
Than that found in still water
Beneath a summer sky.

FRONTISPIECE
Mabel Law Atkinson

A little sapphire mirror-lake
In softly fading light
With tranquil beauty bids me take
A breath of pure delight.

The graceful swans are gliding by
The lilies, fair and pink,
While pine trees reaching for the sky
Grow all along its brink.

Its mirrored beauty murmurs, "Cease
Your restlessness and strife."
It is a perfect frontispiece
To God's own way of life.

Lord, make my life a window for Your light to shine through and a mirror to reflect your love to all I meet.
—ROBERT HAROLD SCHULLER

The calm surface of Peanut Lake perfectly reflects Gothic Mountain in Colorado. Photo by Steve Terrill.

LEGENDARY AMERICANS

Patricia A. Pingry

WINSLOW HOMER

At the 1863 annual exhibition of the National Academy of Design, two oil paintings submitted by an unknown artist stunned both critics and academy members alike. The subject of one of the paintings was the Civil War—not the grand sweep of battle but two soldiers, one standing, one sitting, in front of their tent with the army band in the background. A critic wrote that the force of the paintings was "painstaking labor directed by thought. The delicacy and strength of emotion . . . are not surpassed in the whole exhibition." The most acclaimed of the paintings was entitled "Home Sweet Home," and the artist was a twenty-six-year-old unknown named Winslow Homer.

The Civil War was not only the subject of Homer's first paintings; but the war, in some part, was responsible for his success. Rather than head to Europe to study painting, as was his intent in 1862, the war prevented his going. Instead, Homer took a job with *Harper's Weekly*, where he drew scenes of topical subjects for the magazine. Harper's sent him to cover the war, where he observed the common soldier and drew what he saw.

In "Home Sweet Home," Homer used as his subject a common occurrence at the front. Often, the Union army would play songs such as "The Star-Spangled Banner" or "America"; and the Confederate band, within hearing distance, would counter with "Dixie" or "Bonnie Blue Flag." This unofficial serenade would continue until one band or the other would begin "Home Sweet Home" and the other band would join in as the soldiers stood lost in their reveries. It was this intimate scene that Homer was painting in "Home Sweet Home."

Homer continued to paint the war with "labor directed by thought." He painted a lone marksman in a tree and told the world how the practice of warfare had changed. He painted four Confederate prisoners in front of a Union general, and viewers immediately understood the warring systems of caste and culture that led to war in the first place.

The genius of Homer, for genius it was, lay in his ability to hone in on the spirit of the people and convey a complex but universal meaning and a truthfulness of spirit that represented all of America.

But little is known of Homer's personal life. He was born in Boston in 1836, the second of three sons of Charles Savage and Henrietta Benson Homer. His mother was an amateur watercolorist, and his father was a businessman who encouraged his son's artistic talent. Winslow might have followed his older brother to Harvard, but it was not a school that would nourish his talent.

When Homer was nineteen, he was apprenticed to a Boston lithographer, where he spent his time drawing scenes on lithographic stones for engravings used for sheet-music covers. Homer later described this experience as "bondage," "slavery," and a "treadmill existence." This experience, however, may have strengthened his drawing ability, since it was the most intensive and disciplined artistic training that Homer ever had.

After two years, Homer made his escape and left Boston for New York to be closer to the magazines, especially *Harper's Weekly*. In New York, Homer had a few painting lessons, in which he reportedly learned only how to handle his brush and set his palette. Beyond that, he was self-taught. Homer bought a box of paints, a canvas, and an easel, and set out into the country to paint from nature. For the next five years Homer worked as an illustrator and, presumably, practiced his craft of painting, until the exhibition that would propel him into national prominence.

Homer's life and art fall into distinct phases. In the early days, his oils give us a record of American life. In addition to the Civil War, he painted scenes of country schools, croquet players, women on horseback, boys in fields, African Americans in dignified scenes; and he painted it all with a bright natural light illuminating the subject.

In 1875, Homer left his illustration work. He set up a studio, and, until his death in 1910, not only chronicled American life but also created an original American style of oil painting, turned to watercolors, spoke through his art on the environmental conditions of the Adirondacks, and kept his private life so very private that even today little is known of his day-to-day existence.

When Homer stopped working as an illustrator, he also began to withdraw from society. He became more interested in the design of his oil paintings; and after some time spent in England in the 1880s, his colors were more restrained, his persons more mature, and their enterprise more serious. Critics called his work "classical" and his technique more finished.

By the time of his return from England, Homer was also working in watercolors. As his oils became more serious, his watercolors became fresher and the color more intense. Homer was an avid fisherman and loved the lakes of the Adirondacks, where some of his richest watercolors were painted. It was also here that he painted his social conscience. In a series of paintings, Homer protested the then-current method of hunting deer and the clear cutting of the Adirondack forest. One year after Homer's completion of a particularly compelling oil painting of a woodcutter with no trees left to cut on the side of a clear-cut mountain, the Adirondack State Park was created.

In 1884 Homer, who never married, moved to Prout's Neck, Maine. He settled into his brother's stable and turned it into his home and studio. The winters of Maine were long and severe, and his studio was heated only by a small stove; he wore rubber boots and long underwear to keep warm. Homer had no horses, despised automobiles, and refused to learn to use the phone. He discouraged any visitor who was brave enough to consider making the trip to Prout's Neck. The life suited him, however, and in 1895 he wrote to his brother, "The life that I have chosen gives me my full hours of enjoyment for the balance of my life. The Sun will not rise, or set, without my notice, and thanks."

At Prout's Neck, his subjects were the sea and the men and women who sailed it. His largest and most celebrated works in oil were painted here, and the subjects were the serious ones of life and death. Meanwhile, Homer vacationed in the Caribbean, Cuba, and Florida; and the watercolors he created there are brilliant and the subjects more scenic.

By the 1890s, Homer was so popular and well-known in America that he took on fictional proportions. The few people who actually met him were shocked that he was not a towering figure. Instead he was slight of build and dressed like a stockbroker.

Homer left a legacy of over six hundred paintings and at least half as many engravings that not only chronicle his growth and change as an artist, but also record the changing face of American life. As America moved from the candle and gas-lit nineteenth century into the electrical light of the twentieth, Homer's bright and sunny early oils, painted from nature, gave way to subdued light; his later paintings became more geometric and flat and presaged modernism. Toward the end of his life, the subjects of his oils explored death and eternity. The man who was perhaps our greatest painter of the nineteenth century was almost a recluse, yet Winslow Homer left a body of work that conveys an intimacy and familiarity with life with which all Americans can identify.

DISCOVERY
Pauline Crittenden

On every hand, the mountains stand
As if to touch the sky;
Austere in hue, a titan crew,
Disdaining such as I.

Or so it seemed, when first they gleamed
Upon my wondering gaze,
Their peaks aglow with summer snow
And veiled in purple haze.

But now I know such is not so,
And awe with boldness blends;
For since I've climbed their trails, I find
The mountains are my friends.

THOSE WHO KNOW MOUNTAINS
A. H. Wood

Those who know mountains
Know gay little brooks
Chanting a litany
Not found in books.
Those who know mountains
Know stars and a sky
Rich with the molten
Of sunset's deep dye.
Those who know mountains
Probe mystery trails,
Lost amid trees
Wreathed in mists
And moss-veils.
Those who know mountains
Are fate's chosen men,
Leaving them only
To seek them again.

Mountain lovers appreciate the grandeur of Mount Oberlin in Montana's Glacier National Park. Photo by Carr Clifton.

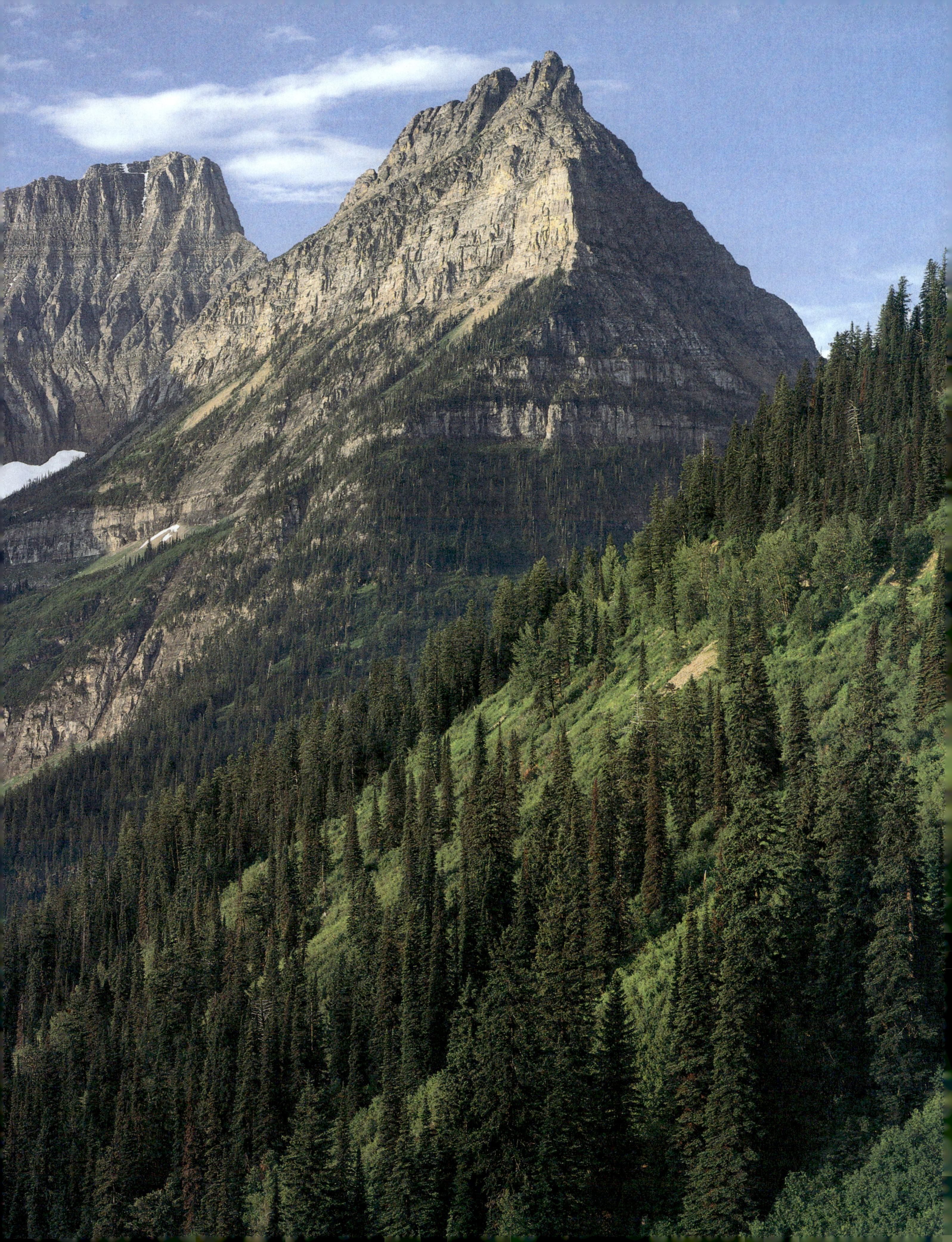

TRAVELER'S *Diary*

ADIRONDACK NATIONAL PARK
NEW YORK

Elizabeth Bonner Kea

During the summer before my husband's graduation from college, he and some friends spent two weeks backpacking in the mountains. He returned to school having had a rustic taste of nature—camping, backpacking, canoeing, fishing—and a wonderful time. In the following years, he often spoke of trying to get away like that again, but each summer slipped by with no vacation. Finally, I decided to surprise him last July with a trip to northern New York's Adirondack National Park. I knew the 6.1-million-acre park would contain all he could possibly dream of in a vacation.

As I planned our trip, I was a little overwhelmed by the size of the park, which covers nearly one-third of the state and contains more acreage than Yellowstone and Grand Canyon National Parks combined. To the north and east of the park were well-trodden trails and interesting attractions set among towering mountains and popular resorts on Lakes Placid and Champlain. I knew my husband would want to be "off the beaten path," somewhere a little rustic and adventurous; but on the other hand, I knew he would also understand my need for a roof over my head and running water! After much researching and a few phone calls to the Adirondack's Tourism Council, I settled on us exploring the central Adirondacks, a region that had it all—stream-fed lakes for fishing and canoeing, hiking trails through dense forests of cedars and spruce, and a rustic yet "civilized" lodging known as Great Camp Sagamore. We could hardly wait for the adventure to begin.

Once we arrived in the park, we agreed to familiarize ourselves with the history and culture of the region by stopping at the Adirondack Museum overlooking Blue Mountain Lake. Located just a few miles from our lodging, the museum offered twenty-three exhibits, including the original locomotive and passenger car that once carried vacationers between Blue Mountain and Raquette Lakes, Adirondack rustic architecture, Adirondack paintings by Winslow Homer and Thomas Cole, and an overview of the region from early exploration to modern tourism. We learned much about the history of the park, which the New York Legislature created in 1892 and continues to strictly protect. In fact, we discovered that New York's constitution designates nearly three million acres as area to be kept "forever wild," safe from development and tourism.

We left the museum, and as we reached our destination of Great Camp Sagamore, our appreciation of the region's history only increased. We learned that in the late 1800s wealthy industrialists attempted to tame what they considered the Adirondack's "dismal wilderness" by purchasing thousands of acres on which to construct "camps," which were actually elaborate lodges and estates. One such pioneer was railroad heir William West Durant, who designed the twenty-seven-building estate of Sagamore. As my husband and I received a brief tour of the grounds, we admired the dark mahogany wood adorning the buildings and marveled at the way all of Sagamore seemed enveloped by the peacefulness of the Adirondack's mountains and sparkling waters.

Artist Winslow Homer captures the unique scenery of the Adirondacks in his painting ADIRONDACK GUIDE. *Image from Museum of Fine Arts, Boston/SuperStock.*

My husband and I felt enchanted by the history and serenity of this region.

For the next few days, we swam and canoed in the pristine waters of Raquette and Blue Mountain Lakes and explored the hidden coves scattered along our way. On foot, we hiked through forests and valleys where Iroquois and Algonquian tribes once hunted. At night, we gazed at a sky unpolluted by city lights and filled with countless stars.

Why had we waited so long to get away like this, we wondered. We had no idea the United States held such a treasure. And as our vacation drew to an end, we both agreed to return to the Adirondacks in the future. With many more lakes, trails, and lodges to explore in the park's other regions, we knew that we had only caught a glimpse of all the beauty Adirondack National Park had to offer.

MUSIC OF THE FOREST

E. Richard Shipp

When you camp in the high hills
And sit beside your campfire
As the sun slips away
And night's purple curtain falls,
There will come to you,
Echoing out of the silence,
The soft notes of violins in the aspens,
The deep note of cellos in the pines,
The joyous flutes of rushing streams,
The crashing drums of waterfalls,
The deep-throated tenor of the wolf,
The high soprano of the coyote,
The low bass of the night owl
In an orchestral symphony.

LAST CAMPFIRE

Mary E. Linton

This was the last night; tomorrow we would go,
And once again this hill, these trees, would know
The silences. Tomorrow this same hill,
Alive with song or reverently still,
Would hold its own communion with the sky.
There was the central fire, flames leaping high,
There was the woods, trees bending close to catch
Some of the radiance that one small match
Brought into being. Gold hung on the leaves,
And night's dark fingers reached from shady sleeves.
We almost felt them touch us as they passed.
Drawn from the shadows to the light at last.
This was the final evening, as we knew
There would be miles and years to travel through.
Then, out of all the voices, your voice ringing,
Starting the very song my heart was singing,
Strong and with courage, "There's a long, long trail,"
Lifted with fervent faith that could not fail.
This was the last night; tomorrow we would go.
But the old, old, hill, long lonely too, would know.
These trees would keep and sing our last refrain
Through other summers, "Till we meet again."

A Toast

Marion Doyle

Here's to every lovely thing—
Drink it from this woodland spring:
Water tasting after pine,
Mint, and myrrh, and columbine,
Winter snow and summer rain,
Spicy fruit and ripened grain.
    Here's to every lovely thing—
    Drink hearty!

Here's to every lovely thing—
Drink it from this mountain spring.
On your knees, you palm the cup,
Lift the crystal water up.
Drink to laughter, life, and love,
To a snowflake on a glove;
Drink to honor, toil, and play,
Night and dawn and high noonday;
To the lowest flower, the tallest tree,
To all beauty's majesty.
    Here's to every lovely thing—
    Drink hearty!

Breathe Deep

Harriet Day

The air is ours to drink without a fee;
God said, "The breath of life I give to thee."
Take leave of man-built rooms, confining, narrow;
Breathe deep and draw the winds into your marrow.
Breath deep the odor of the grass and flowers,
The coolness of the breeze and smell of showers.
Breathe deep the sunshine with its lavish wealth
And fill your soul with glowing, golden health.
What matter if your eager breathing strains
A bluebird note by chance into your veins,
Or if your straining lungs perchance inhale
A tiny whiff of summer's secret ale?
Breathe deep this air from nature's boundless store!
Breathe heaven's breath into your body's core!

Wild daisies and fireweed line Bagley Creek in Washington's Snoqualmie National Forest. Photo by Steve Terrill.

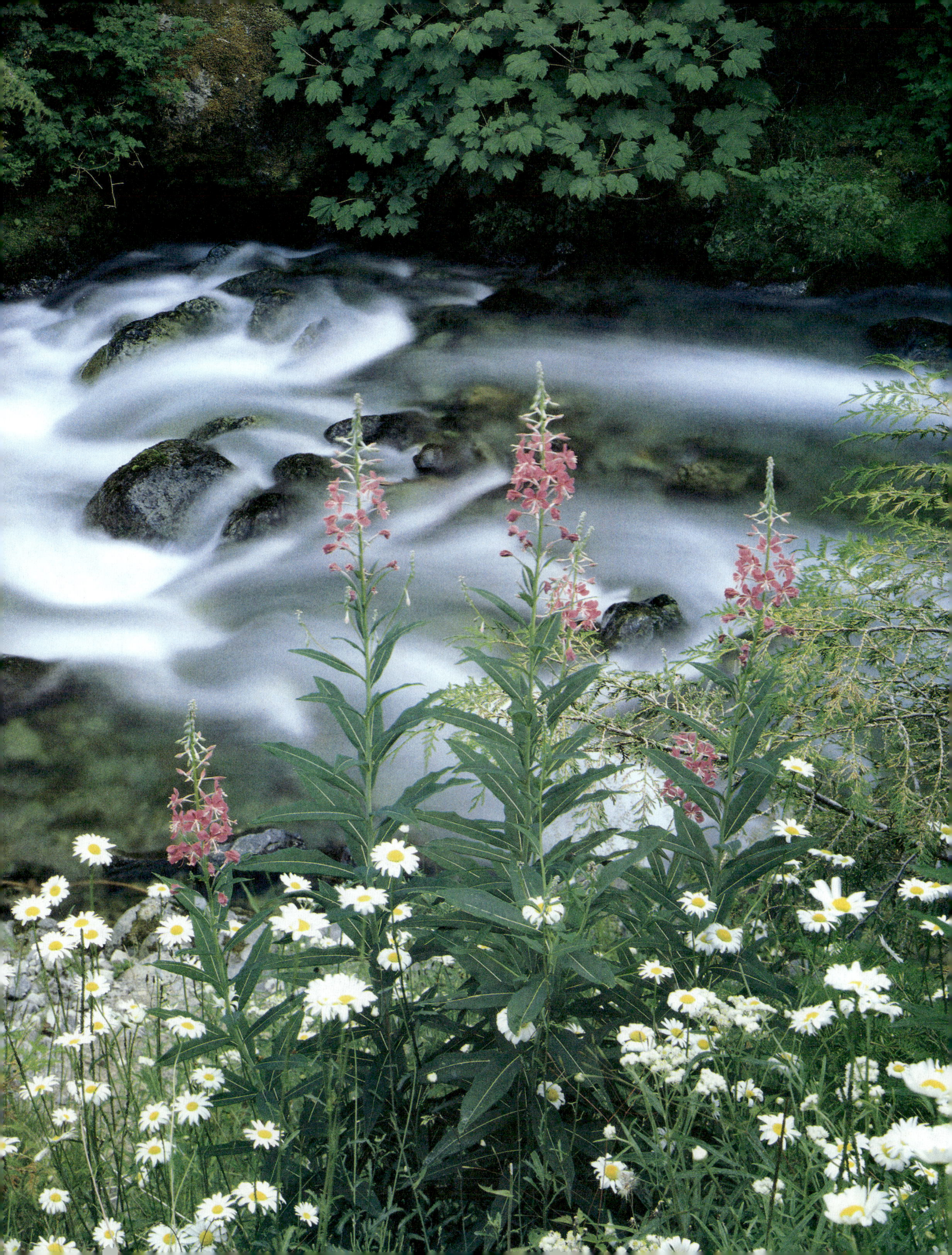

HANDMADE HEIRLOOM

A study of an apple blossom offers a lesson in watercolors.

WATERCOLOR PAINTING

Michelle Prater Burke

As a child, nothing thrilled me more than receiving a new box of crayons, especially the set of sixty-four with the built-in sharpener. I would open the box, place it in front of a clean pad of paper, and dream of the masterpieces I would create with red-orange and blue-green. In third grade, I moved on from crayons to my first art lessons in a makeshift classroom in my school's auditorium, where I crudely imitated charcoal drawings of apples and oranges and displayed my best fruit at the school's art show.

A few years later, I expanded my artistic know-how in the backyard shed of Mrs. Pennington, a kindly woman who held dreams of becoming a great portraitist and finding a protégé among her students. Under her tutelage I wielded real paintbrushes for the first time, and my fruit still-lifes soon took on serious-sounding colors like alizarin crimson and ultramarine blue. When my young hands didn't yield perfect results and I became impatient, Mrs. Pennington would tap her paintbrush on my shoulder and remind me that the goal was not so much the finished piece, but the joy that came from creating. She believed that as long as painting put a smile on my face, I could call myself an artist.

As I pursued my hobby throughout my years at college, I tried my hand at different art media; and sometimes my best efforts resulted in crumpled drawings and wasted canvases. When I felt frustrated with a piece, I recalled Mrs. Pennington's wise words and reminded myself that art was supposed to be enjoyable.

But soon life got in the way, hobbies were overrun by family, and my creativity was limited to painting butterflies on nursery walls. Then several months ago as I watched my son discover each color in a new box of crayons, I remembered how much I once enjoyed putting color to canvas. I decided to revisit my creative side and take an art class, this time with the patience that comes with adulthood.

I considered which art class and medium would best fit my limited time and budget, knowing that I would only have small blocks of time to paint at home and no room for an abundance of supplies. After some thought, I decided on watercolor, one of the few media I had never tried and always admired.

The watercolor technique is unlike any other painting style. Perfected in England in the eighteenth century, this technique allows artists to apply layers of transparent color to capture the light. It is a wonderful medium for anyone eager to take brush to canvas (or, in this case, paper). Although many would-be artists are intimidated by painting and daunted by the number and cost of supplies, watercolor tools are inexpensive and easy to find; and supplies fit in a backpack, perfect for an impromptu painting session almost anywhere. Plus, the basic techniques are fairly easy to learn. Art and craft stores stock plenty of watercolor kits and how-to books that explain the basic tools and brushstrokes, and many communities have facilities which offer basic watercolor courses for those who want personal instruction.

Since the purchase of a book would not give me the discipline to set aside the time to sit down and actually begin painting, I signed up for a watercolor class that was meeting at my church. On the first night of class, I anxiously sat before a large sheet of blank paper with my new paints, brushes, and palette and tried to remember the way Mrs. Pennington, almost twenty years ago, had taught me to hold a paintbrush. The instructor explained the different brushstrokes and then urged the class to practice them by painting rows of waves and arcs on paper. I felt a bit reassured when he asked us to practice painting a few oranges and pears; at least fruit was a familiar topic.

Soon it was time to choose my first project. I sifted through a file full of photographs and decided upon a close-up of an apple blossom, which seemed much more manageable to me than an entire scene. With several pink and green sweeps of the brush and some guidance from the instructor about how to correct my mistakes, I slowly watched the spring flower appear on the white paper. I was pleased to discover that watercolors were more forgiving than I had anticipated. Although I may not have "pulled a perfect wash" (part of my new watercolor lingo), my flower was recognizable; and creating it put a smile on my face that Mrs. Pennington would appreciate.

With several pink and green sweeps of the brush and some guidance from the instructor about how to correct my mistakes, I slowly watched an apple blossom appear on the white paper.

My first watercolor now hangs in an antique frame near my sunny dining-room window. On summer mornings when the light is just right, I plan to create more watercolor pieces to decorate my walls, perhaps one of my prized hydrangea bush or even a curbside view of our family home. I can imagine just such a painting becoming a family heirloom. One day my great-grandchild might look up and remark, "That portrait of the old homestead was painted by Grandma Burke. They say she fancied herself to be an artist." I smile just thinking about it.

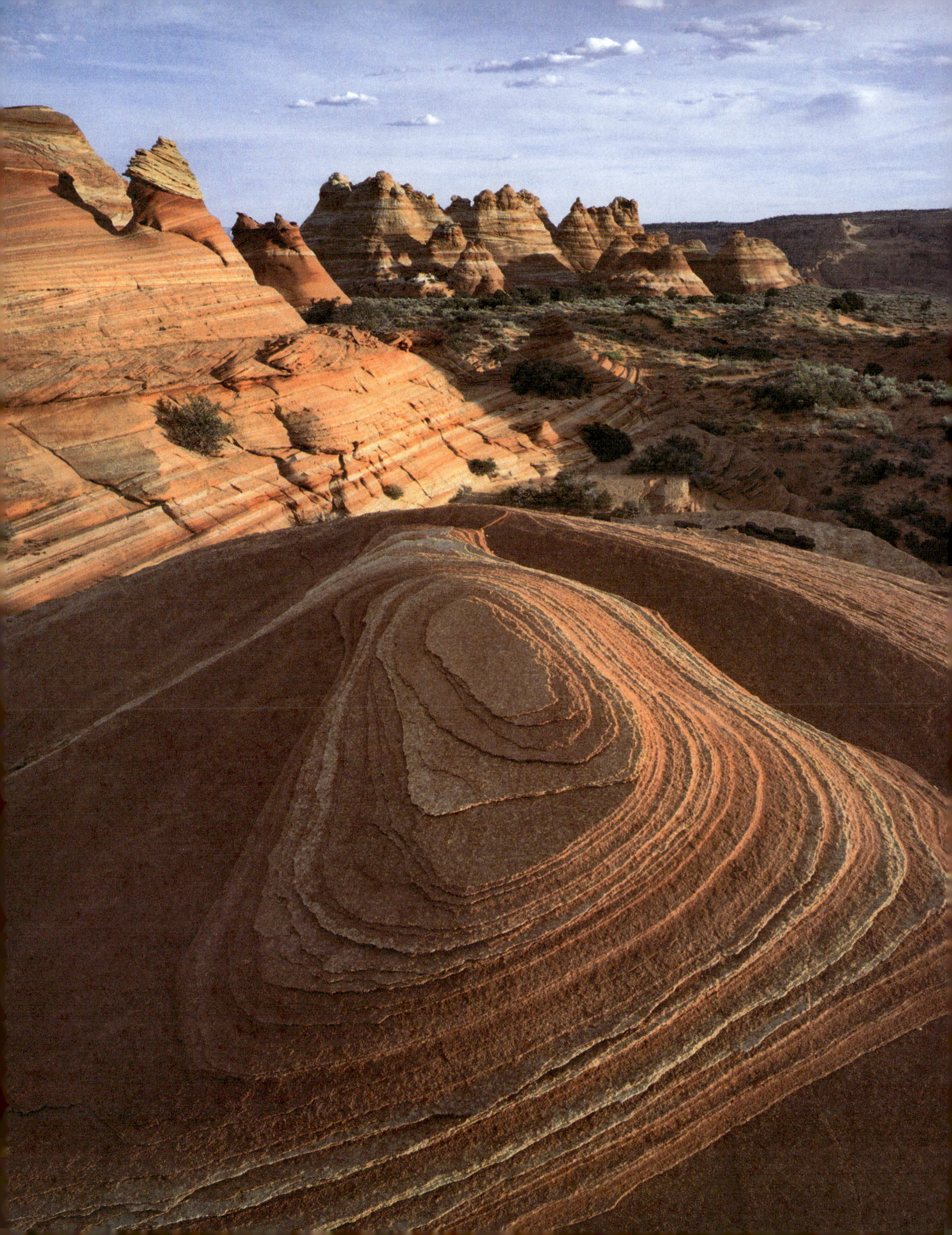

Pioneers! O Pioneers!

Walt Whitman

O you youths, Western youths,
So impatient, full of action, full of manly pride and friendship,
Plain I see you Western youths, see you tramping with the foremost,
    Pioneers! O Pioneers!

Have the elder races halted?
Do they drop and end their lesson, wearied over there beyond the sea?
We take up the task eternal, and the burden and the lesson,
    Pioneers! O Pioneers!

All the past we leave behind,
We debouch upon a newer mightier world, varied world,
Fresh and strong the world we seize, world of labor and the march,
    Pioneers! O Pioneers!

Colorado men are we,
From the peaks gigantic, from the great sierras and the high plateaus,
From the mine and from the gully, from the hunting trail we come,
    Pioneers! O Pioneers!

From Nebraska, from Arkansas,
Central inland race are we, from Missouri, with continental blood intervein'd,
All the hands of comrades clasping, all the Southern, all the Northern,
    Pioneers! O Pioneers!

Eroded sandstone formations create a stunning landscape in Arizona's Colorado Plateau. Photo by Carr Clifton.

Fourth of July Celebrations

Betty W. Stoffel

Let there be prayers as well as great parades.
Let hymns combine with patriotic songs.
Let there be leaders of the future days
With heroes of the past amid the throngs.
Let reverent silence punctuate the noise.
Let God be praised for this great land of ours.
Let sober meditation balance joys
And grave humility mark crucial hours.

Let statesmanship grow from this nation's need.
Let citizenship be equal to these days,
That godly men who gave their lives indeed
Be not betrayed by dull, indifferent ways.
Let joyfulness, not wildness, mark the Free,
That God may find us worth our liberty!

*A family shares its patriotism with a front porch display.
Photo by Darryl Beers.*

*What we obtain too cheaply, we esteem too lightly:
it is dearness only that gives everything its value.
Heaven knows how to put a proper price upon its
goods, and it would be strange indeed if so celestial
an article as freedom should not be highly rated.*
—Thomas Paine

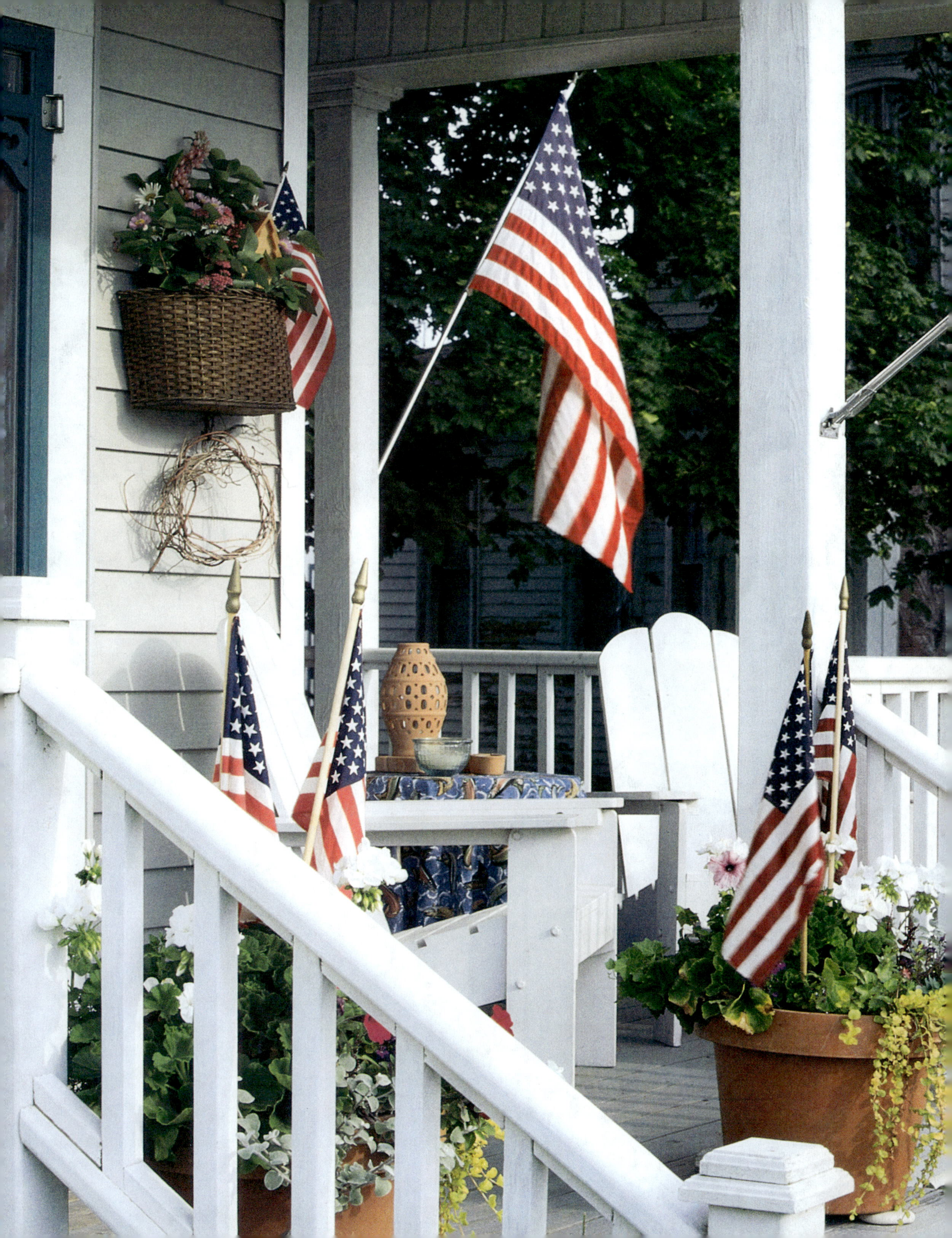

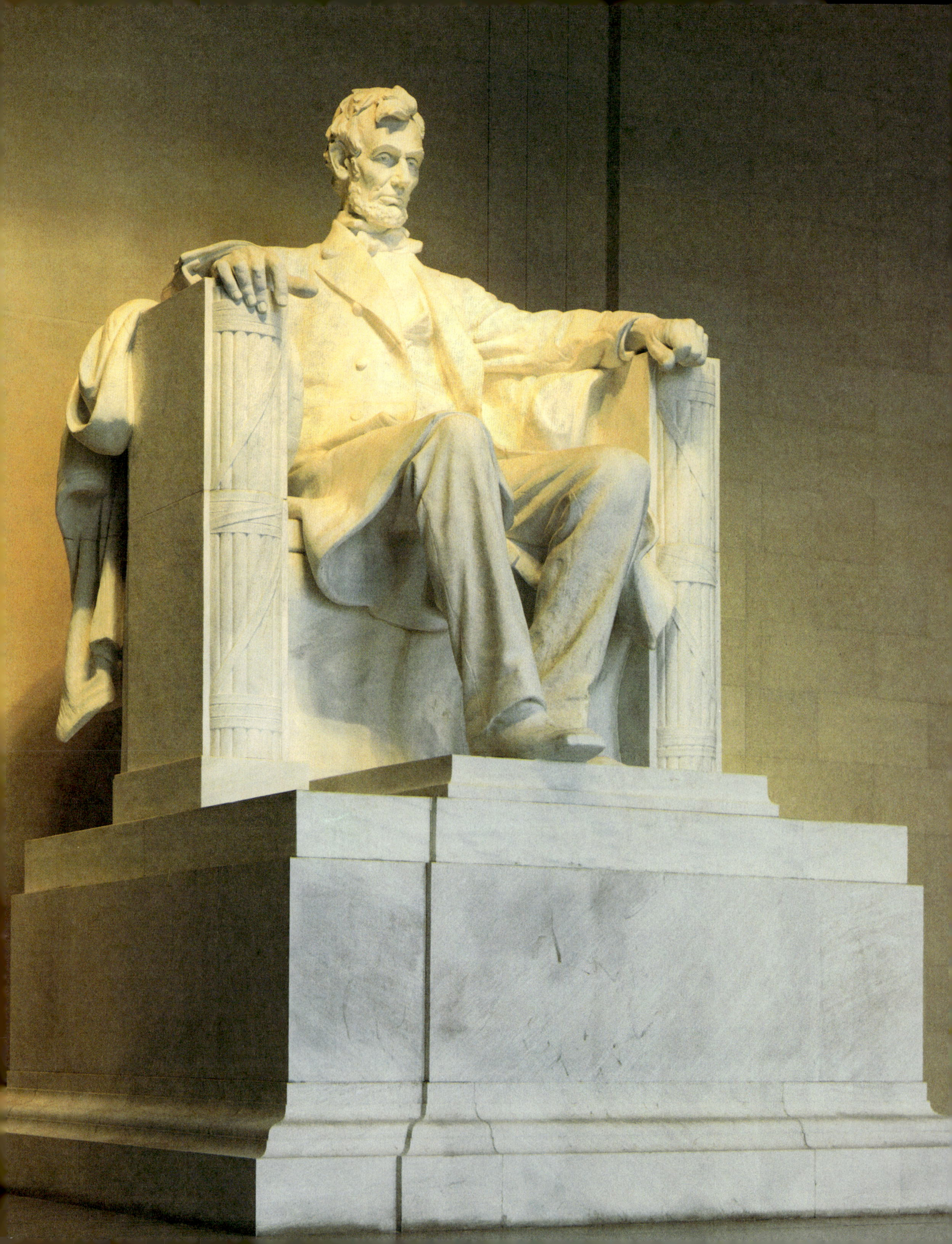

Fourscore and seven years ago our fathers brought forth on this continent a new nation, conceived in liberty and dedicated to the proposition that all men are created equal.

e pluribus unum

Ruth Harris

I was middle-aged and my hair was gray
Before I saw the capitol of our U.S.A.
But I had a feeling of coming home
As I stood on the seal, beneath the dome,
And silently raised my eyes to see
The recorded pageant of history.
And figures out of our nation's past
Were like old friends I had met at last.

Washington, Lincoln, and Jefferson
Looked down in solicitous benison
Upon the problems of laws and men,
Anxious to counsel and guide again
All statesmen who seek the common good
In matters of justice and brotherhood.
Somehow, history and I were one,
And meaning came to Arlington.

Abraham Lincoln looks down at future generations in Washington, D.C. Photo by Jeff Gnass.

. . . we here highly resolve that these dead shall not have died in vain, that this nation under God shall have a new birth of freedom, and that government of the people, by the people, for the people shall not perish from the earth.
—ABRAHAM LINCOLN, THE GETTYSBURG ADDRESS

Readers' Reflections

The Flag
Hope C. Oberhelman
Lubbock, Texas

The flag was waving in the breeze,
All red and white and blue.
The flag of liberty and peace
And justice, pure and true.

The flag was waving in the breeze;
And in my beating heart,
I felt a surge of loyalty
And the will to do my part.

The flag was waving in the breeze,
A symbol of our land,
America, the beautiful;
Long may our nation stand.

The flag was waving in the breeze,
Unfurled and free and wide;
And as it waved, my soul was touched
With dignity and pride!

My America
Mary Lavinia Silvia
Glendale, California

America! My country,
Founded on God's Word;
The victories that she has won
Around the world were heard.

Our flag! It is more beautiful
Than any ever flown;
Our love for it has increased
As America has grown.

The sacrifice our sons have made
Were made for you and me.
God bless my dear America
And keep her safe and free!

Unfurl the Flag
Rev. Robert Goranson
Pekin, Illinois

Unfurl the flag, our nation's flag,
The best in all the earth!
It is the flag that represents
The land that gave us birth.

Unfurl the flag, our glorious flag,
Its beauty we can see,
Rememb'ring where it's been and gone,
The emblem of the free.

Unfurl the flag, our noble flag
That sparks our courage true,
Rememb'ring that it stands today
Just as it did when new.

Unfurl the flag, the flag of peace;
Let cowards cringe in fear.
Our flag has conquered many foes
In lands afar and near.

Unfurl the flag, our honored flag,
And let it ever be
A symbol of our country strong,
Home of the brave and free!

Our Flag
Georgia A. Berkey
Osterburg, Pennsylvania

How gracefully she billows
As she's caught up by the breeze,
Old Glory, known in every land
On earth and distant seas.

Her colors bring a patriotic
Swell to every heart;
We think of her with pride
As our honor we impart.

Her red stripes are for courage
Shown by our heroes strong;
Her white stripes are for purity,
Striving to right the wrong.

And each state floats serenely
On a tranquil sea of blue,
Showing its equality,
A union staid and true.

And as we honor her today,
We pray that God will bless
The Stars and Stripes forever
With freedom and peacefulness.

Editor's Note: Readers are invited to submit original poetry for possible publication in future issues of Ideals. *Please send typed copies only; manuscripts will not be returned. Writers receive $10 for each published submission. Send material to Readers' Reflections, Ideals Publications, 535 Metroplex Drive, Suite 250, Nashville, Tennessee 37211.*

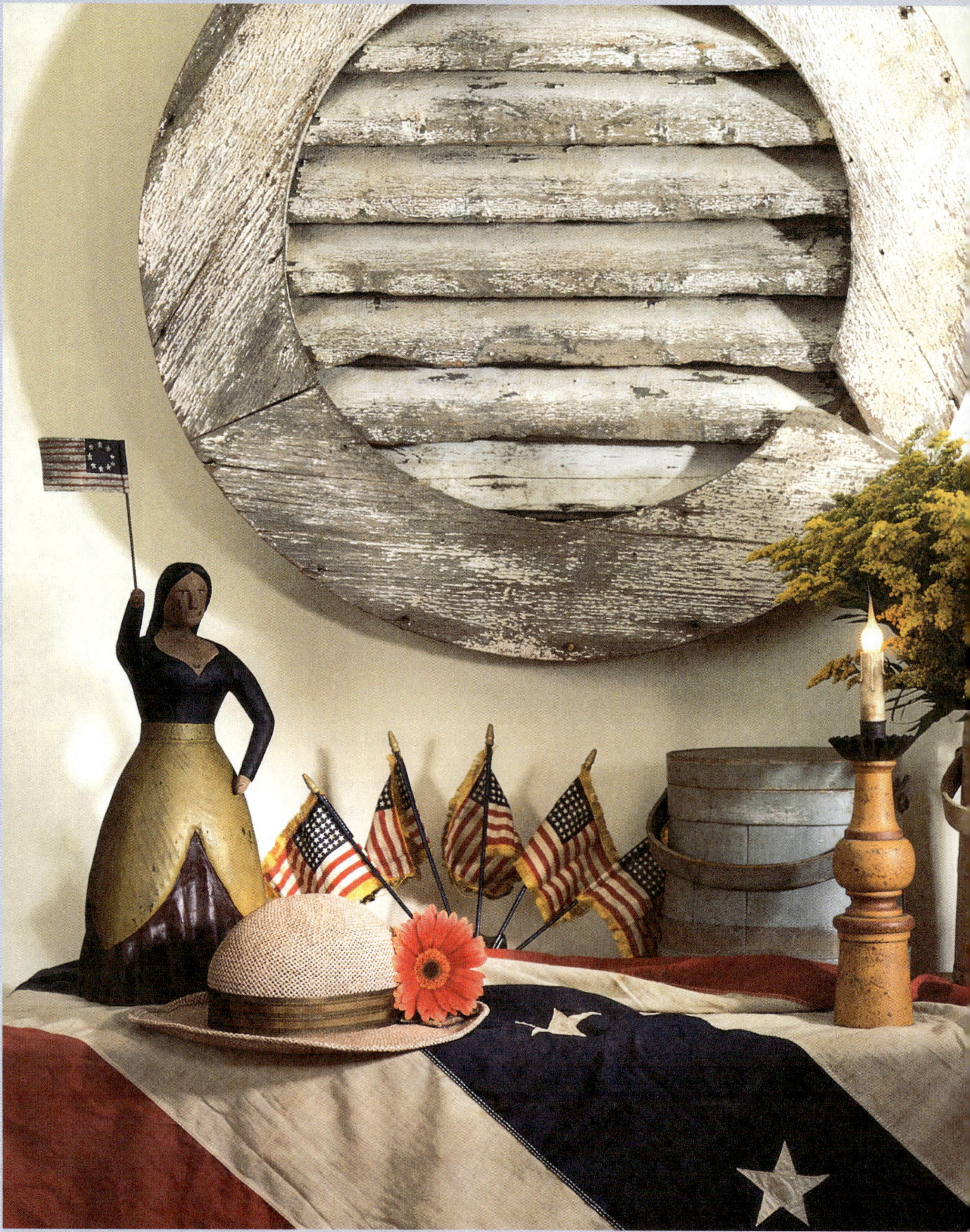

Salute to America

Viney Wilder

Beloved land where freedom dwells
For men of every faith and creed,
Thy hallowed Declaration tells
Equality is in thy seed.

Here to thy rock-bound coast there came
Men who had fled oppression's rod,
Men who would light a sacred flame
To form a nation under God;

Whose dedication was unique
In that its laws would guarantee
The personal right of man to seek
His own religious destiny;

Where freedom's holy lamp would burn
And truth would blossom from the earth,
Where men, at last, would come to learn
The dignity of human worth.

Beloved land forevermore,
May God defend thy holy light
With moral strength in peace and war
And keep thine honor ever bright.

A vintage flag serves as the foundation for this patriotic tablescape. Photo by Jessie Walker.

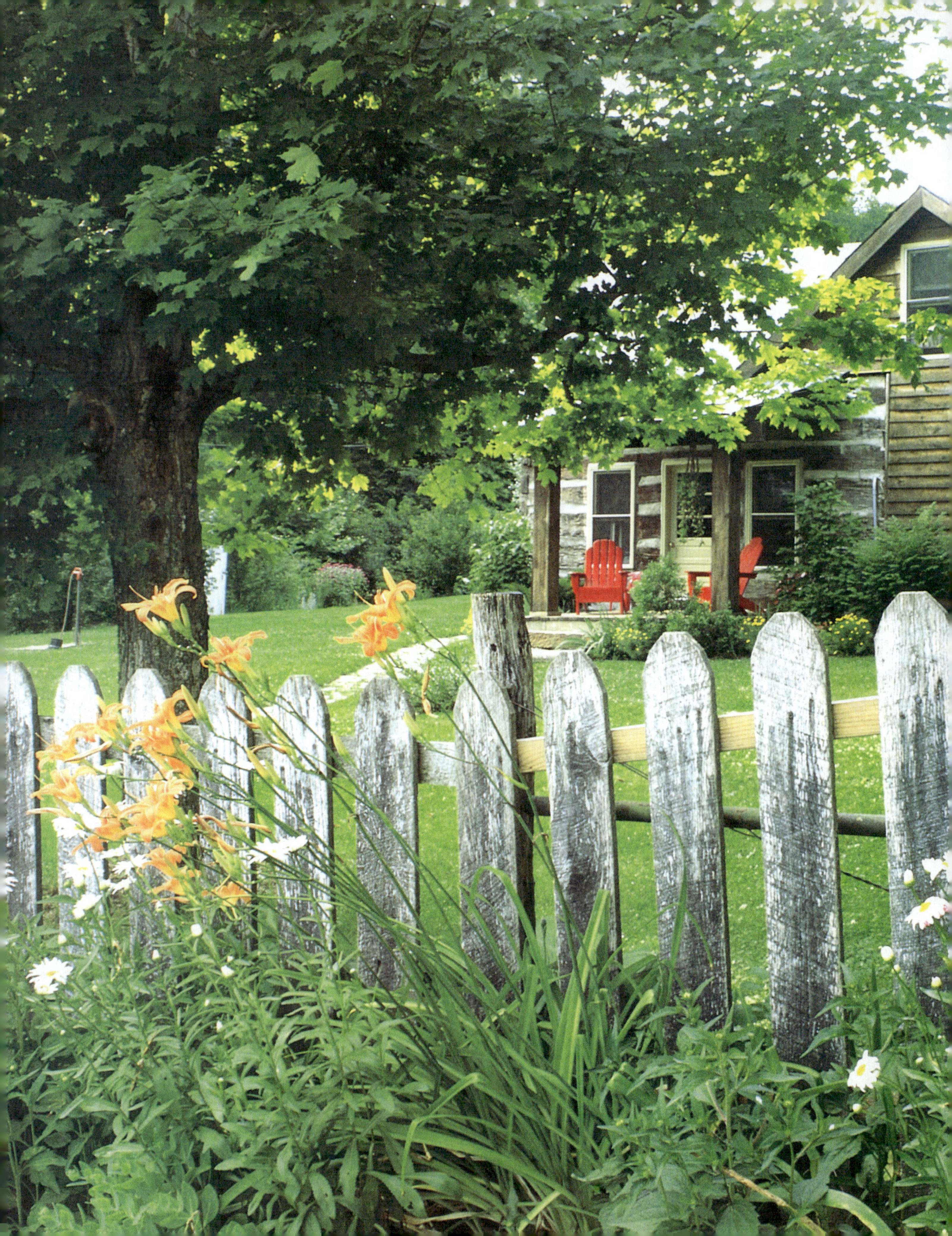

About This Place

Glenn Ward Dresbach

About this place are many circumstances
And certain conditions I should like to know
Will have consideration when I have gone
Reluctantly. The curve where the brook dances
Below the house, I hope will never show
Collected twigs and sodden leaves upon
The polished pebbles. I hope someone will find
The inclination and time to whistle back,
Although imperfectly, the liquid notes
Of these wood thrushes. They seem to appreciate
My answers. I hear them chuckling in their throats
Between calls. And by that wall just behind
The elm may chipmunks never find a lack
Of bread crusts, and no birds in chill winds wait
Too long for crumbs upon the garden wall.
And that red clover by the road is tall
For rabbits to nibble. May it still be so
When they come back in other seasons. Along
The garden, our last steps there will be starred
In flower-patterns. Listen for a song,
Some leaf-stir, some light-whispers as they flow
Through dreams the changing years must not discard.
There are so many things I cannot mention—
But some of them may come to the right attention.

*Daisies and day lilies welcome visitors to a rustic cabin in Story, Indiana.
Photo by Daniel Dempster.*

The Essence

Violet Hall

I would never ask for more
Than to dwell in a cottage deep in thatch,
With climbing roses round the door,
An oaken door with iron latch.

It would cheer and give me pride
To work in a garden of my own,
With my wife, Mary, close beside,
A-shelling peas that I had grown.

And I would paint the garden gate
Or collect the eggs our chickens laid

While Mary baked a seedy-cake
And set the table in the shade.

There we'd share a pot of tea
While shadows crept across the grass,
And loud would hum the drowsy bee
A-plundering every flower he'd pass.

I would never ask for more
Than to sit by the fire when it was cold,
With my old love whom I adore,
The two of us, when I am old.

Farmer's Wife

Mary Fuller Skelton

A storm waits over the land.
With a basket in her hand
my Sarah goes
to gather in the clothes.
Through silent clouds of gray,
one bright shaft penetrates the heavy day,
selects a point on earth with random care,
catches Sarah standing there
and transforms her with Midas' touch,
My Sarah that I love so much.
Once I dreamed beyond this place,
A palace filled with things for me.
But each day went by and only now I
 begin to see
what a blessing on my storm-silenced land
is Sarah, with a basket in her hand.

A farm awaits the day's chores in Summer Day *by artist Edward Henry Potthast. Image from Christie's Images.*

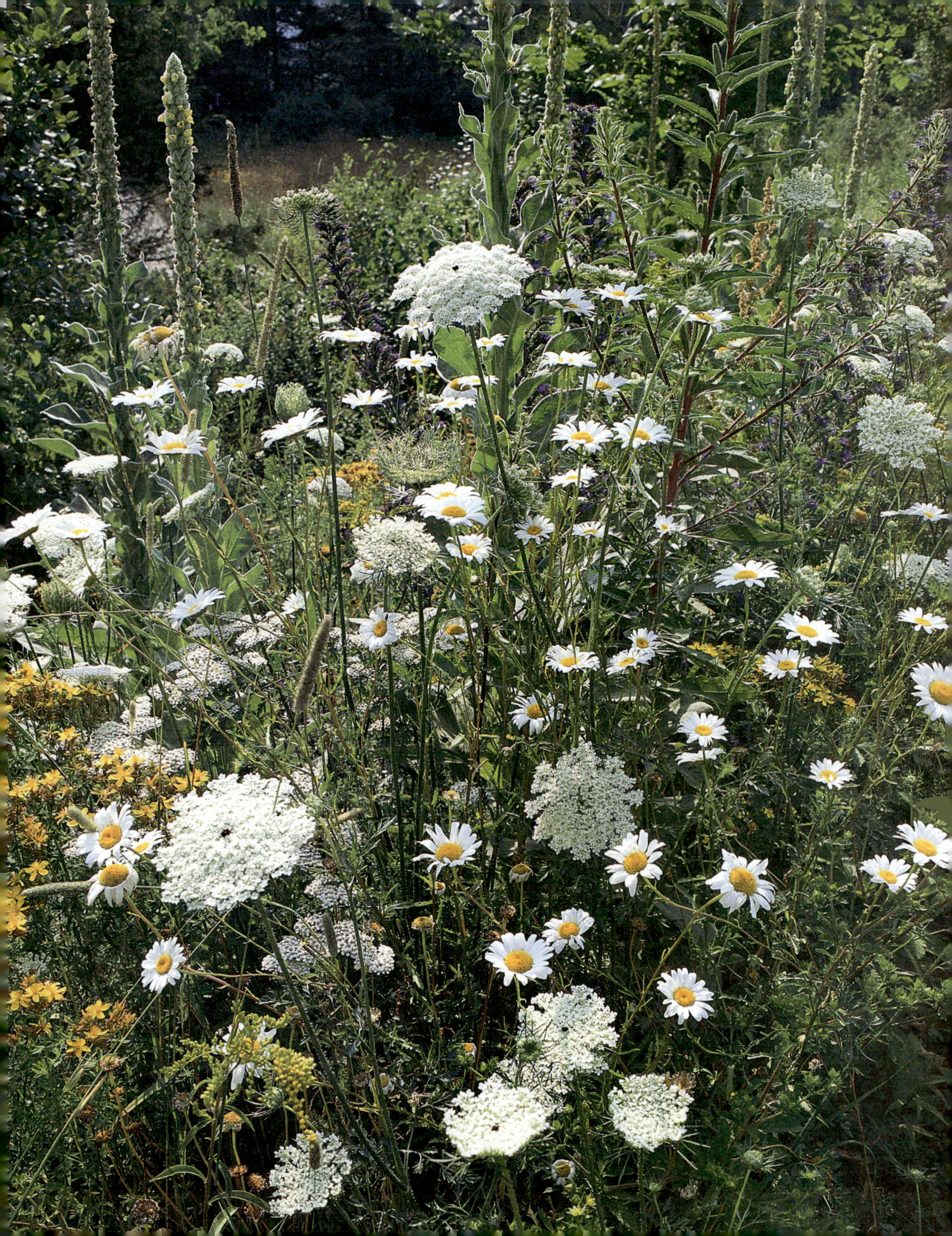

Wildflowers
Beatrice Munro Wilson

I love wildflowers best of all—
The jaunty, common ones that peep
From wayside grasses, halting me,
Forgetful if the way was steep
And hot and long. There's chicory,
Indian paintbrush, blue-eyed grass,
The blooms that greeted pioneers
On prairie trail, in mountain pass.
Did pink owl's clover, buttercup,
Baby blue eyes, pools of sky,
Popcorn flower and queen Anne's lace
Brighten the slow miles creaking by?
Oh, surely so. There's filaree
Clinging close and, marching tall,
Goldenrod by the roughest ways.
Brave wild flowers, I love them all.

Queen Anne's Lace
Frederick K. Ebright

Wild carrot of our childhood days!
The pungence and the poignance spill
Across our years and keep bouquets
Of summer in the mind's eye still.

No Brussels looms could ever spin
A lace so delicate and sheer,
Frost-powdered white, spun cobweb-thin,
Made seemingly of atmosphere.

Acres of foam on inland seas,
Snowfall of stars in summer light,
No garden was as fair as these
Wild tides of tangy-scented white.

Dowry
Florence Foster Hall

Queen Anne's hope chest broken open,
Drift upon drift of white;
Webs by the deftest tradesman woven
Bleach in the hot sunlight.

Queen Anne's linen, sheer and dainty,
Spilled in the market place,
Did ever a bride have gowns so filmy
Or so many yards of lace?

Queen Anne's lace shares its kingdom with daisies and yarrow near Poultney, Vermont. Photo by William H. Johnson/Johnson's Photography.

BITS & PIECES

The heavens are as deep as
our aspirations are high.
—Henry David Thoreau

Delightful Summer! then adieu
Till thou shalt visit us anew:
But who without regretful sigh
Can say adieu and see thee fly?
—Thomas Hood

That golden sky which was the doubly blessed
symbol of advancing day and of approaching rest.
—George Eliot

Green calm below, blue quietness above.
—*John Greenleaf Whittier*

The sky domed above us, with its heavenly frescoes,
painted by the thought of the Great Artist.
—*Allan Throckmorton*

And they were canopied by the blue sky,
So cloudless, clear, and purely beautiful
That God alone was to be seen in heaven.
—*George Gordon, Lord Byron*

All green and fair the summer lies,
Just budded from the bud of spring,
With tender blue of wistful skies
And winds which softly sing.
—*Susan Coolidge*

Every sky has its beauty.
—*George Robert Gissing*

Summer's Golden Days

Nora M. Bozeman

Summer spills her golden days
Upon the earth in lush displays.
She softly sways the apple trees
As songbirds sing sweet melodies.

Summer wears a flower frock
Of goldenrod and hollyhock.
She spreads her magic uncontrolled
In blankets colored bright and bold.

Summer sings her lullabies
To buzzing bees and butterflies.
Silvered moonbeams light the night;
I see a falling star in flight.

God sends the summer scenery,
The birds, the bees, the greenery.
His tranquil nights and sun-filled days
He sends in summertime displays.

Summer

Ernest Jack Sharpe

Of all the seasons, summer is the best.
Vacation time, when one should play and rest,
Enjoying to the fullest nature's charms
Amid the lakes, the woods, the hills and farms.

Where calm lakes, reflecting shore-lined trees,
Pucker up when kissed by gentle breeze,
And, against a cloud-bank way up high,
Swallows crochet patterns in the sky.

When God created seasons we are sure,
Because to it of blessings He gave more
Of nature's beauties than to all the rest,
He must have wanted summer to be best.

In Multnomah County, Oregon, scotch broom covers the ground in gold. Photo by Steve Terrill. Inset: Cultivated sunflowers mimic a sunny day. Photo by Terry Donnelly.

Readers' Forum
Snapshots from Our Ideals Readers

Top left: Michelle Sommerville of Buenos Aires, Argentina, sent us this photo of her nephew, Sasha Blair. Sasha is returning from a walk in his grandparents' eucalyptus woods in Villa Maria, Argentina, where he recently moved from Kansas. Michelle tells us that Sasha loves the outdoor scenery at his new home and is quickly learning to speak Spanish.

Top right: Megan Lauren Howell has found a place to pose during the wood-stove's off season. Four-year-old Megan was enjoying a summer visit with her grandmother, Evelyn Howell of Bismarck, Arkansas. Evelyn states that she loved every moment spent with Megan.

Lower left: Little Morgan Ingamells has found a perfect hiding spot inside one of her mother's antique crocks. This delightful picture was sent to us by Morgan's great-aunt, Allison Volker of Waterloo, Iowa, who loves to babysit Morgan and her new baby brother, Parker.

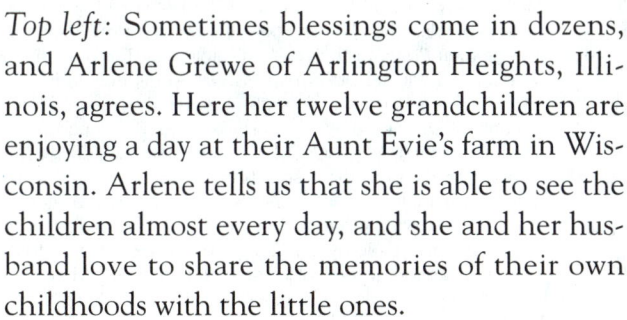

Top left: Sometimes blessings come in dozens, and Arlene Grewe of Arlington Heights, Illinois, agrees. Here her twelve grandchildren are enjoying a day at their Aunt Evie's farm in Wisconsin. Arlene tells us that she is able to see the children almost every day, and she and her husband love to share the memories of their own childhoods with the little ones.

Top right: Theresa Panezich of Cape Coral, Florida, shares this photo of her nine grandchildren posing on their great-grandfather's tractor. Standing in front are Sierra and Lauren; and across the top are Jessica, Tim, Alicia, Jennifer, Sidney, Casandra, and Ryan. Theresa and her grandchildren were enjoying a family reunion and traveled from Ohio, Pennsylvania, and Florida to be together.

Lower right: Knowing the family picnic is this afternoon, three-year-old David Emerson is working hard to bring a watermelon home from the neighborhood market. Good thing he has his little red wagon to help. This snapshot was sent to us by David's father, of Kensington, Maryland.

THANK YOU Michelle Sommerville, Allison Volker, Evelyn Howell, Arlene Grewe, Theresa Panezich, Paul Emerson, Diana Davis, and Dr. and Mrs. John C. Kistler for sharing your family photographs with *Ideals*. We hope to hear from other readers who would like to share snapshots with the *Ideals* family. Please include a self-addressed, stamped envelope if you would like the photos returned. Keep your original photographs for safekeeping and send duplicate photos along with your name, address, and telephone number to:

Readers' Forum
Ideals Publications
535 Metroplex Drive, Suite 250
Nashville, Tennessee 37211

Above: Diana Davis of Indianapolis, Indiana, sent us this photo of her granddaughter Brittany Davis (age two) and her playmate Angelia. Wearing their red, white, and blue, the girls are ready for a lakeside Fourth of July celebration at Diana's family home.

Right: Dr. and Mrs. John C. Kistler of Kiln, Mississippi, tell us that their first grandchild, John Cameron Kistler, is quite a happy baby. We can see that he is patriotic as well! Five-month-old John lives with his parents in Slidell, Louisiana, but loves to visit his grandparents as often as he can.

ideals

Publisher, Patricia A. Pingry
Editor, Michelle Prater Burke
Designer, Travis Rader
Copy Editor, Amy Johnson
Contributing Editors, Lansing Christman, Pamela Kennedy, Nancy Skarmeas, and Lisa Ragan

Acknowledgments

BRABHAM, MAUZON W. "A Father's Prayer" from *Prayer Poems*. Copyright © 1942 by Abingdon-Cokesbury Press. Used by permission. BURKET, GAIL BROOK. "Along the Pasture Stream" from *This Is My Country*. Used by permission. COFFIN, ROBERT P. TRISTRAM. "A Father Is a Strange Thing" from *The Collected Poems of Robert P. Tristram Coffin*. Copyright © 1935 by Macmillan Publishing Company, renewed © 1963 by Margaret Coffin Halvosa. Reprinted with the permission of Scribner, a Division of Simon & Schuster, Inc. GUEST, EDGAR A. "Best Tribute." Used by permission of the author's estate. HOLMES, MARJORIE. An excerpt from "Carry Me Back to the Farm" from *You and I and Yesterday*. Used by permission of the author. JAQUES, EDNA. "Down-to-Earth Things" from *The Golden Road*. Copyright © in Canada by Thomas Allen & Son Limited. PIERCE, DOROTHY MASON. "Sprinkling" from *Sung Under the Silver Umbrella* (p. 40). Reprinted by permission of Dorothy Mason Pierce and the Association for Childhood Education International, 17904 Georgia Avenue, Suite 215, Olney, MD. Copyright © 1935 by the Association. STOFFEL, BETTY W. "Fourth of July Celebrations" from *Moments of Eternity*. Used by permission. TREMBLE, STELLA CRAFT. "Summer Comes" from *Center and Circumference*. Used by permission. Our sincere thanks to the following authors whom we were unable to locate: Mabel Law Atkinson for "Frontispiece"; Agnes Davenport Bond for "An Old Rail Fence" from *Old Rhymes, Old Times*; Frederick K. Ebright for "Queen Anne's Lace"; Florence Pedigo Jansson for "No Blue Can Match the Sky"; Sheila Stinson for "Idiosyncrasy" from *Warmth for Heart's Winter*; and May Smith White for "Hill Farm Reclaimed" from *Upon Returning*.